Once Upon a Christmas

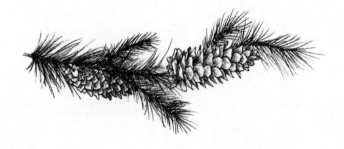

Once Upon

a

Christmas

A COLLECTION BY

Pearl S. Buck

Illustrations by Donald Lizzul

THE JOHN DAY COMPANY / *New York*

A number of the stories and articles in this volume originally appeared in the following publications: *Good Housekeeping, Family Circle, Ladies' Home Journal, American Weekly, Chatelaine,* and *Suburbia Today.*

The John Day Company, 257 Park Avenue South, New York, N.Y. 10010
An Intext Publisher

Published on the same day in Canada by Longman Canada Limited.

Printed in the United States of America

Library of Congress Cataloging in Publication Data

Buck, Pearl (Sydenstricker) 1892–
    Once upon a Christmas.

    CONTENTS: To an American family at Christmas.—
Once upon a Christmas.—Christmas miniature. [etc.]
    1. Christmas stories. I. Title.
PZ3.B8555On [PS3503.U198]   813'.5'2   72–2410

DESIGNED BY STANLEY S. DRATE

Contents

To an American Family at Christmas

Ah, Christmas! It goes back far, far into my memory, into the earliest years of my childhood. Christmas was the time when we were really American —my parents, my little sister, and I. There were many other festivals which we celebrated with our Chinese friends during the Chinese moon-year. There was even an English festival, the Queen's Birthday—Queen Victoria, of course—which we celebrated with the handful of English who lived in the British Concession, a strip of walled land along the Yangtze River. Our city, the provincial capital of Kiangsu Province, was a treaty port and that it had a British Concession was the result of the Opium Wars, each of which the English won because the Chinese had centuries ago established the principle of international peace by rejecting aggressive warfare.

Curiously enough, Christmas each year of my childhood began with a Christmas Eve party for all non-Chinese children, this party being given by a kindly English lady in the British Concession. I enjoyed the party because it was elaborately generous as to food and gifts, but my enjoyment was hampered by two facts: one, that we had to go in fancy costumes, which tortured my naturally shy self; and, second, all my real friends were Chinese and I resented their exclusion. Mrs. Tamplin's parties were the beginning of each year's Christmas, nevertheless, and so continued until her Commissioner husband was retired or sent elsewhere—I do not know. But I do remember the magnificent house, the soft carpets and rich furniture, and the great glittering tree.

Our own tree was small and much less loaded with gifts. But the gifts included those for our Chinese household and the things we children had made for our parents, at which they always expressed the proper appreciative surprise. And of course theirs for us, brought presumably by Santa Claus from faraway America, via Montgomery Ward, from whom my parents ordered once a year such necessities as we could not buy in our Chinese city. When we ceased to believe in Santa Claus I do not know, but my inventive mother made the transition easy—so easy, in fact, that my first narrative poem was written on the subject. The poem was lost long ago, and I remember now merely my agony at my mother's requiring me to read it aloud to a group of her friends. Perhaps I even tore it up afterwards—I was capable of that, I fear.

Christmas dinner was of course an event. Turkey was unknown, but we had roast goose, with trimmings, preceded by the once-a-year-only oyster soup, a favorite dish of mine to this day, but rare in those days for oysters were imported in tin cans from a foreign country—Australia? England? Perhaps even America! But wherever, that Christmas oyster soup surpasses, in my memory, all subsequent ones.

We hung up our stockings, and found them always delightfully overflowing. These could be emptied and enjoyed before breakfast, but the tree only after breakfast and after my father, in his grave, beautiful voice, had read the Christ story. The tree came after that, usually a pretty holly tree which an enterprising villager cut for us each year from the nearby mountains, bringing also two great loads of lovely, richly berried holly, one at each end of his carrying pole. Chinese holly is the most beautiful in the world—the leaves prickly but glossy and the scarlet berries abundant. I speak with a small authority for in my Pennsylvania home grounds, I grow varieties of holly from many countries.

From such memories of my Chinese childhood, it is no wonder that when I had an American home of my own, complete with husband and children, every Christmas was as joyous as we could make it. The living room chimney was wide enough for Santa Claus and even his reindeer to come down. We helped him, of course, the children by trimming the tree, the parents by filling stockings, after children had been coaxed to bed. These parents worked at their Santa Claus job each Christmas Eve until long past midnight and heroically rose early the next morning to express the proper surprises.

But why go on with what every American family knows? We threw in a few extras by going to New York ahead of time and standing ankle-deep in snow and slush so that the children could see Macy's great Thanksgiving Day Parade, and we had a standing order for the best box at the Radio City Christmas performance, and there were Christmas plays and concerts in Philadelphia, nearer home.

All that is left of these years, however, when the children are grown, married and making their own Christmas joys, is the handful of Christmas stories I wrote for my children in those days, for my grandchildren now and, indeed, for all children. I told my children many stories when they were small enough for bedtime stories, and each year they chose one to make into a book. The Christmas stories, of course, were always special and they are collected here in this book. Are they true stories? People always ask that question and I always answer—well, yes and no. Take *The Christmas Ghost,* for example. Our early Pennsylvania stone house has a ghost, as all properly ancient houses have. His name is Old Devil Harry, and though his remains are buried—"extra deep," I am told—in our village churchyard, his ghost continues lively about the house and the vast red barn. I have lived more than thirty-five years in the house and have never seen him, though at night the century-old beams groan sometimes in a strangely human fashion. Our old gardener, however, now gone and buried in that same churchyard, always insisted that the ghost of Old Devil Harry did walk every Christmas Eve at midnight from the big red barn to the bridge, to meet the ghost of a former crony with whom he used to get drunk each Christmas Eve. The gardener's little house stood, and still stands, just beside the bridge from which one can see the barn, and the old gardener said he always saw the ghost each Christmas Eve come down the hill to the bridge. Naturally and so inevitably, *The Christmas Ghost* became a story. As for *Christmas Miniature,* our yellow cat did chase and nearly caught a tiny mouse one Christmas Eve and that I saw myself.

As for the other and the more grownup stories, they grew out of life itself, as all my stories do. The circumstances of life change with the years. Houses that once were full of life grow lonely. But new friends are made, new experiences take place, and wherever the place may be and whatever the circumstance, the miracle of Christmas remains, living and true, so long as one lives and loves life for its own sake.

Wherever you are, then, my reader, my friend, may this small book bring you joy, though it be but for a moment, or a day, or for as long as you live!

Danby, Vermont
1972

Pearl S. Buck

Once Upon a Christmas

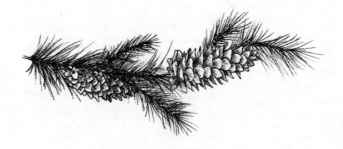

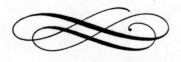

Once Upon
a Christmas

It is Christmas Eve. The house is still, the stockings hung at the chimneypiece, the holly wreaths in the windows, and I have put the last gift under the Christmas tree. I treasure these final few minutes, each year, before I go upstairs. I feel my home warm about me, alive with past memories and present life, fulfillment of yesterday and anticipation of tomorrow. For strange and wonderful events have happened to me at Christmas and I have come to expect the unexpected, some new joy above other joys, the over and beyond. I wonder what it will be this year?

And while I wonder I remember, and I do not know why, another Christmas, long ago, and far away from here. I think of a night before Christmas, like this one. I was very young then, newly married to a man I did not know well enough. In that China, at least in the Chinese circles in which my family lived, it was difficult for a girl to see a young man alone or often. Letters, yes, but there were few meetings before we were married. Now I was alone with him at Christmastime, we two the only Americans in a small ancient city in north China, and I was trying not to be lonely. My parents were coming to spend Christmas, however, and how eagerly I looked forward to that! For days I had been making elaborate preparations, the first I had ever made by myself: a wild goose instead of the turkey not to be had in our remote part of the world; eight-precious Chinese pudding, made of glutinous rice, and eight kinds of sweet dried fruits, instead of plum pudding; heavenly bamboo with its green leaves and scarlet berries instead of holly.

Then, on the very morning of Christmas Eve, a telegram announced that my mother was not well enough to come, and my father must stay with her!

Suddenly Christmas was empty and the celebration forlorn. Of course I tried to hide my disappointment, but the day dragged and I was glad when evening came and I could light the kerosene lamps—there was no such thing as electricity in our city. I played Christmas carols, I remember, and we talked, we two, of Christmas in our childhoods, his in a farmhouse under snow in America, mine in a Chinese house in a tropical climate, until at last it was time to go to bed.

I could not sleep, I remember. After an hour or so, just before midnight, I got up and went to the window in the living room, and I saw a star shining above the city wall, but very far away. It was at this moment that I heard a knock on the front door, a soft, hesitating sort of knock. Who could be there at such an hour? Bandits lurked in our area, and perhaps I should not open the door. But I did open it. A small boy stood there, a small Chinese boy, ten years old, he said later, but looking five or six. He was very thin and he was in rags, but what I remember to this day are his eyes. He had enormous dark eyes in a thin angelic little face, the forehead high and the chin pointed beneath a beautiful calm mouth. Indeed, the expression of the face was unusual. Pale and emaciated, that child's face was tranquil, confident, untroubled. He did not speak. He simply stood there, looking up at me.

"Who are you?" I asked in Chinese.

"I am no one," he answered. He spoke with a pure Peking accent.

"But what is your name?" I asked.

"I have no name," he replied.

"Where are your parents?"

"I have no parents."

I stared at him as though he had dropped out of the sky. Perhaps he had.

"Where did you come from?" I asked next.

"I come from nowhere," he said.

"And you are going nowhere?"

"Nowhere."

"Then why come to me?"

He shook his head, unable to answer this, and he kept looking at me with those great steady luminous eyes.

As for me, I stood in a sort of trance. Who was this lovely solitary child?

4

A beggar? But why here at our door, and why tonight at midnight?

"Come in," I said. "You must be hungry."

He came in silently, and I saw then how thin he was and how travel-worn. He was trying not to shiver, and he went to the fireplace, where the last coals were still red and held out his hands to the warmth, delicate little hands, but black with dirt, and his hair was brown with dust. Evidently he had been walking a long time, and he must have suffered some sort of shock since he remembered nothing.

In silence I took him to the bathroom and bathed him clean and cut short the legs and sleeves of a pair of flannel pajamas and put them on him, and tied a strip around his narrow waist to hold him together. Then I gave him food, scrambled egg and bread and milk from a tin can. He did not know what milk was, and he smelled it politely and set it aside.

"Will you have tea?" I asked.

"Please do not go to trouble," he replied.

I made tea and he drank it thirstily. Then I prepared a bed for him on the couch in the living room and sat by him until he went to sleep. I went back to bed, and for some reason I, too, was able to sleep.

In the morning when I went into the living room he was already awake. He was sitting on the floor, cross-legged, looking at the tree with quiet pleasure.

"Do you remember who you are this morning?" I inquired.

He gave me a shy lovely smile and shook his head. Then he said quite simply, "I have come to live with you."

And that was the way it was. He shared our Christmas Day and I did not miss anyone. Since the shops were open that day like any other, I took him out and bought clothes for him and he behaved as though he had always lived with us. We named him Noel, and if any of our Chinese friends and neighbors knew where he came from or who he was they did not tell us. They simply declared they had never seen him, and he never remembered anything of his life before that Christmas Eve, except that he was tired and hungry and someone told him to knock on our door. Of course I know he was not the Christ Child, or anyone like that, but he reminded me of that Child, then and always until he died. He died very young, too, and in a way one could say he died for others.

5

That was years later. Meanwhile he lived with us and went to school, and grew up. I do not remember that he was ever a trouble. He liked to study. People were drawn to him but he made no close friends. He seemed always apart, pleasant and helpful, but apart.

He grew into a tall, slender, brilliant young man. He wanted to be a doctor and he became a good one, one of the rare ones who treated the poor and the helpless as carefully and lovingly as he did everyone else. No one ever quite understood him. I think I did not, either. He seemed utterly selfless, wholly devoted to the sick. He remained silent, meditative, his eyes still large and calm. Those delicate hands of his became the hands of a skilled surgeon. It seemed he would go on living that way forever, and we accepted him, all of us, relying on his goodness.

Then the war came and China split in two. Everywhere the Communists were fighting the Nationalists, and in our city both sides were angry with him because he treated the wounded whatever side they were on. The Communists won and we, with all other Americans, had to leave China. I wanted him to come with us, I begged him to come, promising him more medical schooling. But he refused, smiling and gentle.

"I must stay here with my own people," he said. "They will need me more than ever."

I remonstrated. "But will the Communists let you be yourself?"

"I am only a doctor," he said. "They can scarcely object to that. They need doctors."

So we parted, I feeling that I was leaving a younger brother. At first we wrote letters, but later it seemed better for both if we did not write—he suspect because he had letters from America, I suspect because letters came to me from China.

Then I heard how he had died. A friend escaped from China and told me. He spent himself, my friend said, living alone and overwhelmed by work. He was the only doctor in hundreds of square miles, and people came to him from everywhere, especially wounded soldiers, and these from both sides. He was warned by the victors that he must treat only their wounded, not the wounded of their enemies. He smiled and said nothing and went on treating anyone who came to him.

One night he was called out of his sleep and, going to the door, he saw

6

three men there, ordinary men, it seemed. They asked him to come to visit a very sick man a few doors away. He buttoned his coat and went with them at once. When they turned the next corner they shot him and he died instantly.

This is all I know. But it is not of his death that I think tonight. It is of him, as I saw him that Christmas Eve, long ago, a little child from nowhere, nameless, who came somehow to my door.

Christmas
Miniature

It was the night before Christmas. Sandy had done his best to sleep. He had gone to bed early and he had tried not to think about Santa Claus or the tree downstairs or his stocking hanging by the fireplace or whether there would be a bicycle behind the tree. It was hard but he had tried.

"The sooner you go to sleep," his little mother had told him, "the sooner Santa Claus will come. You don't want to keep him waiting, do you?"

"On such a cold night, too," his big father had said. "His toes might get frost-bitten."

They had hurried him into the tub, they had scrubbed him fast and hard, laughing all the while, for he was six years old and on other nights he took his own bath. They had rubbed him with the red bath towel, red for Christmas, and buttoned him into his red pajamas, red for Christmas again. They had tossed him into his bed as soon as he had said his prayers and covered him up in his warm red quilt. When his father opened the window, the snow blew in.

"A white Christmas," his little mother cried and clapped her hands. She was still quite young, her yellow hair all curly about her face.

Sandy was her big boy. He had a room to himself while his baby sister, Dilly, slept in her crib in the nursery. Her name was really Elizabeth, but when she was born she was so pretty that her father had shouted at the sight of her:

"Oh, what a dilly!"

That was what he had shouted and her mother had laughed.

"Dilly she is," she had said, "and Dilly we'll call her."

Dilly, of course, was already asleep when Sandy was finally tucked in, kissed, chucked under the chin, and left alone to go to sleep, too.

He had gone to sleep, not at once, but after he had told himself that really he must not think about Santa Claus, who was waiting out in the snow, his toes getting frosted. He slept a long time, so long that when he woke, he thought it was late. The night before Christmas is always long, much longer than other nights, or so it seems every year. Sandy lay in his bed, wondering what time it was. The house was still, and on the floor beside the open window the snow had made a drift. Maybe he had better get up and shut the window. He pushed back the covers and crept out of bed and shut the window. Of course the right thing to do was to get back into bed, but he did want to know what time it was. He could tell time, not by minutes, but certainly by hours and half hours and quarter hours, on the old grandfather clock in the hall at the foot of the stairs. He'd go and look at the clock and see what time it was and then run back to bed.

When he was five years old, Sandy's kind mother had given him a flashlight to use if he felt afraid in the night, which he really wasn't any more, although he had been when he was small, but she let him keep the flashlight, in case. He used it now, not because he was afraid, which he wasn't at all, but to make a round spot of light go in front of his feet like a lantern. Down the stairs the light shone steadily ahead of him. The door to the nursery was closed, and so was the door to his parents' room. Oh, how huge and quiet a house is at night! Not a sound did Sandy hear, not a footstep, not even his own, for his red pajamas covered his feet and besides there was carpet on the stairs. Down he went, step by step, following the light as though it were a star leading him. When he had taken the last step, he lifted the flashlight and let it fall upon the face of the old clock. The man in the moon, painted exactly above the XII, looked back at him, and there the hands of the clock pointed, both together. It was midnight, and the night before Christmas!

Had Santa Claus come? That was the question. The door to the living room was closed. On Christmas, as Sandy remembered, his father shut the door into the living room so that Santa Claus could be private.

"Santa is a sort of artist," his father had said. "He likes to be left alone while he does his work. He wants to get everything just right."

Maybe it wouldn't matter if Sandy just opened the door a little crack and flashed his light through that crack, to see if Santa had come or not? For if not, then indeed he must hurry straight upstairs to bed and shut his eyes tight, so that Santa need not wait any longer. Very well, then! Sandy opened the door just enough to put the light through into the living room. There was the tree where it always stood for Christmas, between the fireplace and the picture window. Ah ha, Santa Claus had come! The tree was beautiful, shining with tinsel and bright balls, and under it—well, the heap of presents was higher than ever, although every year his father pretended to grumble.

"Good gracious, Elaine," he grumbled—Elaine was the mother—"it'll take us all day merely to tear off ribbons and paper."

And what was that gleaming so red from behind the tree? Could it be a—bicycle?

Sandy had no time to look. For suddenly he saw a horrid sight. Snips, his yellow cat, was crouched under the tree. The light glittered on his eyes and they looked like marbles of fire. But Snips was not looking at Sandy. He was looking at a very small mouse who stood helpless with fright just inside the crèche, under the tree. The mouse had run there, thinking perhaps that it was a safe place to escape the cat, who seemed, to a tiny brown mouse, as big as a jungle tiger. While Sandy stared, Snips crawled forward on his stomach to the very door of the crèche, and there he lay, enjoying the mouse before he caught her and ate her.

Sandy was horrified. He loved Snips, who was a playful cat; but a cat is a cat, and Snips, while he had learned only to look at birds and switch his tail longingly, could never resist a mouse. Though it was Christmas Eve, he had sauntered about the house as usual, and seeing the heap of presents under the tree, he had investigated. Thus he had surprised the mouse, who had smelled cheese. There was a cheese, a nice Danish cheese, wrapped in silver paper and

ribbon, for Sandy's father loved cheese, and insisted that he must be given a whole round cheese every Christmas, or he would pout all day. He always got a cheese and so no one knew whether he would pout all day or not.

It was this cheese that had tempted the mouse. She was a mother mouse, and behind the wainscoting behind the couch she had a nest of babies, each one no larger than the end of Sandy's thumb. Since she was often hungry and tired, she had left them asleep when she smelled cheese and, coming out, she had found the package and had already nibbled off a corner of silver paper when Snips smelled mouse. Cheese he disliked but mouse he loved, and so he had appeared and scared the mother mouse so that her little knees shook. The crèche was near and into the crèche she had run, taking shelter behind the tiny manger, wherein lay the tiny image of the Christ Child. Mary, the mother, knelt beside the manger, and Joseph knelt beside her.

The mouse had no time to see them. She crouched behind the manger, keeping very quiet until she thought the cat Snips had gone away and then she stood on her hind legs and lifted her head above the manger to see if she were safe. Oh, what horror indeed! Far from being safe, she was in the greatest danger. There, preventing all hope of escape, the great cat crouched at the entrance to the crèche. He had but to put out his paw and she would be caught in his curving claws. And her babies, lying so innocently asleep, what would become of them? They would starve and die. She would never see them again.

The big cat stared at her. He, too, was thinking she could

not escape. He would tease her for a while and then, when he was tired of playing, he would eat her up in a minute. Rather thin she was, a mere mouthful for a big yellow cat, but a nice mouthful. Mouse meat is delicious for a cat, very tender, the little bones easy to crunch. Snips began to purr.

In the crèche, peeping above the tiny manger, the mother mouse heard that purring. It sounded like rumbling thunder in her frightened ears. Who could hear her voice even if she squeaked? And who helps a mouse? She was quite alone. These small silent people in the crèche were hardly bigger than herself. They did not move. Perhaps they, too, were afraid of the big cat. Though it was no use—oh, no use at all—still she could not keep from squeaking. She was so afraid, so desperate.

"Please—please—please—"

That was the way her little squeaks sounded. But no one could hear her. The purring roar of the cat was much too loud.

It was at this moment that Sandy's light flashed upon the crèche and he saw what was going on.

"Snips!" He called, but not too loudly. After all, Santa might still be in the chimney.

Snips did not turn his head. He kept on purring and gazing at the mother mouse. So what could Sandy do but push open the door and squeeze through into the living room, Christmas Eve though it was? He kept his light steadily upon the crèche and just as Snips put out his paw to snatch the mother mouse, Sandy put in his hand first and caught her and saved her.

"Me—yow—yow," Snips howled.

17

"I don't care," Sandy said. "The idea of your catching a mouse on Christmas Eve! And right in the crèche!"

The mouse, however, did not know she was saved. She felt herself caught in a warm hand and she thought she must be in a trap of some sort. She had the kindest heart in the world, but she had never been held in a hand before, and in her fright she opened her mouth and bit the end of Sandy's thumb. It was a very small bite, not enough to hurt, for the mother mouse's teeth were scarcely bigger than the sharp end of a pin. Still, it was enough to surprise Sandy and he dropped her and she ran under the couch.

There he might have lost her except that Snips, cross because he had lost his tidbit, ran after her. Then Sandy followed Snips, and pushing the couch away from the wall, he saw the cat peering into a small hole in the wainscoting. He let the light flash into the hole, and now he knew why the mouse had been in such haste. There upon a soft nest of cotton wadding, which of course the mother mouse had pulled from inside the couch, were five baby mice, all pink, and each no bigger than the end of Sandy's thumb. And curled around them, already feeding them and cuddling them, was the mother mouse. She did not move when the bright light flashed upon her. Perhaps the light dazed her, perhaps she knew that the hole was too small for either Sandy or Snips to reach her. Perhaps she just hoped that she was safe.

"Ow—wow—wow," Snips said sadly. He knew that the hole was too small for him to get through. Even his paw was too big to reach in and bring out a mouse. There was nothing to do but wait. He crouched down and switched

his tail and his jaws quivered while he watched.

"Ow-wow-wow," he moaned.

"Be quiet," Sandy said. He kept looking at the little family in the stolen nest. This house was not only his home, then. It was the home of another family, too, a mouse's family, mother and children, and a father mouse, who was probably out hunting for food.

"Snips, you leave them alone," he said sternly. And he stooped and took Snips under his arm and held him, legs and tail hanging down on one side and head on the other.

"You come upstairs with me, Snips," he said. "I'll shut the door so you can't get out again tonight."

So, with the cat hanging on his arm, Sandy pushed the couch back to its place.

He was just about to leave the room when he thought of something wonderful. Wasn't it wonderful that he had waked just at twelve o'clock on Christmas Eve, had come downstairs, not indeed to peep at the Christmas tree but only to see what time it was, and then peeping, after all, not at the Christmas tree but just to see whether Santa Claus had come and gone, and then that he had seen, quite by accident perhaps, the mother mouse hiding in the crèche? And suppose he had not come down, and suppose Snips had caught the mouse and had eaten her, leaving blood there upon the floor of the crèche, right where Mary knelt beside the little Jesus, how sad that would have been! And what of all those mouse babies, none bigger than the end of his thumb, waiting for the mother mouse, who would then never have come back? How could it have been a Merry Christmas for them? For the babies would have died, wouldn't they, and his mother would have found them sooner or later, and the sad story be told? Oh, wonderful that he had waked at Christmas midnight, and led by the light, have come to save the mouse family!

He paused by the crèche, thinking these thoughts, and the light shone in upon a peaceful scene. The hay, really only a handful of dried grass from the lawn, was piled behind the manger, and there the tiny image of Jesus slept. And Mary and Joseph knelt lovingly by, their hands folded. Above the crèche was the tinsel star, and it caught the edge of Sandy's light and shone down upon the scene like a real star of Bethlehem.

Well now, he must go back to bed. He tried not to look behind the tree for it was not fair to see the presents before morning, but his light quite by accident caught the edge of something that was certainly a red wheel. He turned away firmly. No, no peeping! He tiptoed out of the living room, closing the door after him, and still guided by the light, he climbed the stairs and went to his room and shut the door. Only now did he put down Snips, the cat, who was getting heavy. Then he got into bed.

"Naughty Snips," he said, looking down on his yellow cat, who was plainly planning to get into bed with him.

Snips laid back his ears and switched his tail. Naughty?

"Me—yow—yow," he protested.

"Well—ell," Sandy said, yielding, "come along then. I suppose you don't know any better."

He pulled up the covers and tucked the red quilt around Snips, too. A cat is a cat, and Snips couldn't help being interested in mice.

"All the same," Sandy said, "I'm glad the light happened to flash into the crèche just at that minute."

And he went to sleep without any trouble at all. Santa Claus had come and gone. The baby mice were safe with their mother. And in the crèche the holy family waited for Christmas morning.

Christmas
Story

She tied the last ornament to the tree. It was the small silver harp they had bought when they were honeymooning in Ireland six years ago this Christmas, she and Sean.

"Mistress O'Malley," he had said, "will you accept the gift of a harp from a true son of Ireland? I wish it were gold, set with diamonds, to be fit for you, darlin'—but at least it's a harp. You can even play on it."

He had touched the miniature strings with his fingers and she heard their faint and faery music. Remembering, she touched them now, and again she heard the tinkling music, as though a harp were playing afar off . . . The dog snarled softly in the next room.

"Davy!" she cried. "Have you taken Mimi's puppy again?"

"It's my puppy!"

He came in as he spoke, her five-year-old son, the image of Sean, his father. High above his head he clutched in both hands a worn stuffed toy, a rag puppy, once white and now gray. Mimi, the French poodle that Sean had given her on her birthday three years ago, leaped at it madly, and whined.

She snatched the toy away from Davy. "With all your toys," she scolded, "why can't you let Mimi have this old puppy?"

"It's mine—it's mine," he wailed. "I want to sleep with it, in my bed."

"Don't be silly! You haven't slept with it for months. Let Mimi have it."

She tossed the toy to the poodle. Then she pulled her son down on the couch beside her and ruffled his hair. He had Sean's blue eyes and black hair—yes, and Sean's bright, rebellious face.

"It's a dirty old toy," she said. "Santa Claus will bring you lots of nice new ones tonight."

To her surprise, he burrowed his head into her breast and sobbed suddenly. She pushed him away and looked at him. "Why, Davy, the idea! Crying? For shame!"

"I don't want Mimi to love the puppy!"

What she would have said to that she did not know, for at this moment the telephone rang and when she took up the receiver, she heard Sean's voice.

"Hello, Cynthia! This is Sean."

"I still know your voice, Sean," she said, coolly.

He laughed, and she remembered that, too, his gay big laugh.

"I'm thinkin' I might drop by for a few minutes with a present I've bought for Davy, since it's Christmas Eve and all."

He waited and when she did not answer he hurried on. "I won't stay, I can assure you."

She saw Davy's face at this moment, lit as though a candle flamed inside him.

"Very well," she said abruptly, "though he's just about to go to bed."

"Bathe him and put on his pajamas," Sean said. "Then you can pop him in as soon as I've gone, a matter of half an hour or so, at most."

She heard him put up the receiver before she could reply, an old trick of his when he wanted the last word. Even the telephoning was a trick. When in October they had decided their marriage was over and she had told him so, he had kissed her gently on the top of her bowed head and then had left the house without a word. Ten minutes later, when she was crying bitterly, the telephone rang, and he was pouring out talk.

"Cynthia, darlin', I don't blame you—not a bit, indeed! Were I in your boots—your darlin' shoes, I mean, your little high-heeled golden slippers —I'd do the same. I'm a wastrel and a failure, totally, and on top of it, all else you said is gospel true except one thing. It's true I've lost three jobs in the year, on account of my own waywardness in not bein' able to stick to them. But I've not kissed another girl like you said. I'm not above wantin' to, for a minute or so, I'll admit, when I've seen the look in her eye at me, but I'm faithful to you, I swear—for it's you I love—"

She had interrupted the flow. "Sean, I've tried—"

He had broken across her voice. "Sure you've tried, but I'm a disap-

26

pointment to you. In fact, I'm a disappointment to myself. And you're right that a separation is entirely what should take place, for a while anyhow. I'd thought of it myself. Truth is, nothing's been any good between us for a long time, has it? Though I thought when we bought the little house—''

There his voice choked and the tears had rushed to her own eyes, too. The house, this adorable house, their dream ever since Davy was born, where they were to live happily ever after, had become the loneliest place on earth. Bought? They hadn't bought it. The mortgage was as big as the house. But she had not yielded. Davy must have some sort of life, and she could not forgive Sean again. Before she could say so he had hung up the receiver.

Davy's voice broke across her thoughts.

"Is Daddy coming?"

She looked into his eager face. "Yes, after your bath. Let's hurry. He can't stay long."

He danced ahead of her and in spite of herself, she felt a vague excitement. Sean was coming! She longed for it and dreaded it. When he was away from her, she could keep her heart cold to him. But the moment she saw him, the magic would work, the magic of his smile, his voice, his warm, cajoling ways. She'd missed him beyond telling, but she had been resolute. She had her old job back, executive secretary to Mr. Robbins at the United Steel Company, and she was saving for the next payment on the mortgage.

And what had Sean been doing these three months? Who had looked after him? He could never look after himself, a careless fellow who forgot to put on his overcoat on a cold day, forgot to eat, forgot what time he'd said he'd come home. Ah, that had been torture, never knowing when he'd come home for meals or even to sleep, and that air of innocence when he did come, as though he were surprised that she could be annoyed!

She drew the bath, she found Davy's pajamas and then decided on a new pair she'd planned to put under the tree tonight—yes, and the new red bathrobe and slippers to match.

"I'm giving you these presents early," she said, "so that you'll look beautiful—"

"For Daddy or for Christmas?" he asked.

27

He was out of the tub now and dripping and she caught him and dried him thoroughly.

"For Christmas," she said and then, "maybe a little bit for Daddy, too."

She put the new pajamas on him and the red bathrobe and slippers and brushed his hair and he was so beautiful that she was frightened. What if Sean wanted him? What would she do if, when the divorce came, Sean would insist on her sharing him half the year? What would she do without Davy even for a single night? She hugged him suddenly and so hard that he pushed himself free and accused her.

"Don't love me so much! You hurt me—"

She felt a strange clutch of the heart. Sean had said something like that—

"You love me too much, darlin'. You don't leave me free—"

She had cried out in agony and anger. "If you really loved me, you wouldn't want to be free."

He had looked at her strangely. "Ah, there's the difference between us!"

"Let's light the tree," she said now. "Then we'll be ready."

They went into the living room and she lit the tree and they sat down properly on the sofa to wait. In the corner of the room that was especially hers, the dog Mimi lay curled about the stuffed puppy, her eyes warily upon Davy. Would he or would he not threaten her treasure?

Silly dog, Cynthia thought! She'd take the puppy and throw it away except that Mimi had such a fixation on it. The creature would moan and refuse to eat, would weep actual tears, the way she had done last week when Davy put the puppy on the book shelf. Cynthia had given it back again, against Davy's shouts of rage and loud sobs. Such a storm over nothing! The whole house was upset.

The doorbell rang. Davy leaped to open the door and she followed slowly. It was decent of Sean, she thought, not to use his key, but to ring the bell as any stranger would. He could be sensitive about small things, however selfish about big ones.

"Daddy!"

She saw her son throw himself upon his father and suddenly she felt a deep thrust of pain in her bosom. He was here—he was here. Their eyes met, he smiled, and she felt the old pull at her heart.

28

"Davy!" she said sharply. "Stop being silly—"

"He's not silly, Cynthia—he's only glad to see his dad, eh, boy? Gad, but I've missed him! And you, darlin'!"

He threw off his coat and let it drop on a chair, just as he always had, and she suppressed the habitual impulse to snatch it and hang it up in the coat closet.

"And how are you?" Sean said. He looked cruelly healthy, she thought, and even happy, as though he enjoyed his life. And of course he did enjoy his life, wherever it was. And with whom? That was the eternally unanswered question.

"I'm well," she said calmly, "and I can see you're fine, yourself."

"I've a new job," he said, "and I'm working day and night at last."

"Day and night?"

"In the theater," he said. "Don't laugh now, Cynthia, but the truth is I never knew before what I was meant to be, and now I know. I'm an actor —born, they tell me."

"I daresay," she said in a small wintry voice. "It's what you've always been—nothing but an actor, wherever you are."

He laughed, "Pick on me, darlin'! It makes me feel at home."

She stopped the rush of anger in her. "How did you come to know you're an actor?" she asked in her calm, cold voice.

She sat down on the couch again and took up her knitting, a blue sweater she was making for Davy. He sat beside her, Davy cuddled in his arms.

"It was an accident altogether. I was readin' the want ads one day as usual, and I saw the notice that actors were wanted for a new play, especially an Irishman, so I said to myself there's never a man more Irish than me, and so I went to the place mentioned and spoke my best brogue that you've been tryin' to cure me of since you first laid eyes on me, darlin', and it was the very thing they wanted for the play—a handsome Irishman with a brogue strong enough to float a ship on, which I have, as you know. And with my first week's pay, which was today, I've bought two presents, one for you, and one for Davy."

He fished in his pockets and brought out two packages, one very small, and one larger.

29

"Open yours," he said.

"I don't want a present," she said.

"Sure you do," he coaxed. "At least you will when you see what it is. You'd take it from a stranger, it's that pretty."

"But I have no present for you, Sean, because I didn't think you'd be back."

"Why should you give me a present, darlin'? The trouble and all that I've been to you, it would only hurt my feelin's if you gave me a present. Open it, there's a girl, if only to give me a bit of Christmas joy before I go." He glanced at his watch. "And go I must, for we're having a show tonight, special."

She untied the ribbon reluctantly, not knowing how to refuse when he said he must leave so soon, and there in the small velvet box she saw an old-fashioned brooch, a spray of silver flowers whose petals were tiny pearls, a dainty thing, and just to her taste.

"Oh, Sean," she said under her breath. Then she flew at him. "But how could you spend so much on a bauble? The payment on the mortgage comes up in a week—"

He put his hand on her mouth. "It's Christmas. The mortgage can wait a bit, surely."

"That's where you're wrong," she cried. "It's not honest—decent people pay their bills. That's why I went back to the office. I couldn't stand owing money everywhere."

"And who stays home with Davy in that case?"

She looked at him, taken aback. She'd laid herself open to that attack, but it was cruel of him, just the same. He returned her look with malice and mischief.

"I take care of Davy," she said. "He's in kindergarten in the mornings and—"

"Not so fast," he said. "He's half mine. And I'm not lettin' even my half-son be neglected while you gallivant at a job. Fact is, it'd be easy for me to take care of him altogether. I'd be with him all day and put him to bed before I leave for the theater, when I'd get somebody to keep an eye on him."

"I'd never trust you," she said bitterly. "An actor! What kind of a job

30

is that? When the play closes, how long will it be before you get another? Who'd stay with Davy while you're tramping the streets, looking for another? I'll die before I let you have him!"

They heard a snarl from the other room.

Sean leaped to his feet. "What's that, in God's name?"

"It's only that silly Mimi."

She could not finish, for Davy screamed, a choked, frightened cry. Neither of them had noticed when he left them. He'd slipped away while they quarreled. They ran into Davy's room, where he slept and played. There on the floor they saw him. In his hand he clutched the toy puppy and at his throat was the poodle, Mimi.

Sean gave a great shout. "Come off, you beast!"

He seized the dog in both hands and tried to shake her loose from the boy. He might as well have seized a small wild jackal. Mimi the gentle one, Mimi the loving playmate, had become a raging morsel of insane energy.

"I'll wring her neck," Sean muttered, "if I can get her still for a second—"

Cynthia snatched the puppy from Davy's hand and threw it across the room. "Here, Mimi!" she cried.

Instantly Mimi turned from the boy. She took the puppy gently between her teeth and crawled to a corner and began to lick it.

Sean lifted Davy to his feet. "Let me see—"

Davy was crying, terrified, but he was not hurt. In all her fury, Mimi had not been willing to set her teeth in him. Four tiny marks, not breaking the delicate skin, were all that could be seen. Cynthia kneeled beside him and held him in her arms.

"Oh, Davy, I told you this would happen."

"What is all this?" Sean demanded.

She looked up at him, her arms about the sobbing boy.

"It's Mimi," she said. "I wish you'd never given her to me."

"Mimi?" He sat down on Davy's bed. "Come here, let me see your throat."

He examined the childish throat again and smoothed the dents. "Impulse to kill," he muttered, "but she was too good to go through with it. A loving heart—in spite of her instincts."

31

"It's been horrible," Cynthia said. "She's been out of her mind about that rag puppy. She thinks it's alive. She washes it and sleeps with it and watches over it. And Davy insists on taking it away from her."

"Because it's my puppy!" Davy wailed.

"She thinks it's hers," Cynthia said sharply, "and with all your other toys, can't you—"

"Be quiet a minute," Sean said. He lifted his son to his knees, coaxing. "But why, Davy, do you need this little toy puppy? You don't play with it any more. It's a baby toy. Couldn't you give it to Mimi?"

"No." Davy said. "I want it."

"For what, Davy?"

"I want to burn it up."

"Why?"

"So Mimi can't have it."

"And why shouldn't she have it, Davy?"

There was no answer. Leaning his head against his father's shoulder, Davy wept in soft, shaking sobs.

"You don't know," Sean said gently. "And Mimi doesn't know why she wants that puppy, either. It's mixed up between you. Is that it, Davy?"

The boy nodded.

"Shall I tell you why, Davy?"

The boy lifted his head, suddenly interested. "Do you know, Daddy?"

"I can guess," Sean said. He looked at Cynthia. "I do know, in a queer sort of way. Mimi's only a poodle, but she has her feelin's. What she wants is a puppy of her own, the way your mother wants you. Mimi's dreamin' of a little puppy of her own and not havin' it she wraps her dream on the rag puppy. She dreams it's alive. She dreams it's her family. She doesn't know it's just the old rag puppy that you used to play with. She's all mixed up on account of lonesomeness. And you're mixed up because you're lonesome and you think she doesn't love you any more, now she has the rag puppy. She used to play with you, and now she just wants to take care of a puppy of her own. And you can't bear it."

"Oh, for heaven's sake, Sean!" Cynthia cried under her breath.

"Don't be sharp with me," Sean said. "I'm speakin' of natural feelings, dog and boy, and they're the deepest truth. Man and woman, too—if we don't have the reality, we dream up something and fasten our dreams on anything that's handy."

He rose as he spoke and Mimi growled again. She was in the corner encircling the rag puppy.

"You little idiot," Sean said, "don't growl at me! You can have your rag puppy until you have a puppy of your own."

He turned to his son. "As for you, Davy boy, it's time you had playmates of your own, too, somebody more than a dog. You should have brothers and sisters."

"Don't go, Daddy!"

The boy's voice was a cry, a passionate call.

"I have to, my dear," Sean said. "I have a sort of job—a sort of night job."

"But you'll come back?"

Sean hesitated. "It depends on your mother and you."

The child whirled on her. "I want my Daddy back!"

The two of them were against her. She saw it very well, and she did not put it beyond Sean to use the dog and the rag puppy and the child to arrive at this very point of demand. She looked at him, trying not to yield. And he stood smiling down at her.

"It's a family situation, darlin'," he said. "You see what comes when a lady like Mimi turns into a vixen because she has no proper family of her own. She should have had her family long ago but we've been so busy with our troubles. You can't run against nature, darlin', not even when you get mad at your own mate, and throw him out of the house for his many wicked ways . . ." He stooped and kissed her cheek.

"Oh, Sean," she whispered. "I can't go through with it all again."

"Does that mean you've stopped lovin' me?"

She turned away from him, hiding herself from the yearning temptation of his eyes, his face, his beautiful voice.

"Look at me," he said.

She felt his hand under her chin, twisting her face to his.

"I'm makin' love to my lawful wife, Cynthia," he said. "Do you love me? Tell me."

"Of course I love you," she said, trying to twist her head away. "But that doesn't mean a thing."

33

He let her go and straightened his shoulders. "It means this to me, Cynthia. I'll try better. I'll do better. I'll be my old self now and again, I daresay. Still, the three of us, father, mother and child—children, someday —it would be natural and good for us all to be together and not this miserable way of livin'—me in a hotel room, and you here without me, and Davy fightin' for the love of a poodle dog, lackin' the two of us."

"Oh, Sean, you're making it all up!"

"Am I, sweetheart? Look at me and say it."

"Oh, Sean," Cynthia said. She looked up into his eyes and suddenly she laughed. "If you knew how silly you look, standing there being noble!"

"Sure, if it makes you laugh," he said, "then I'm happy to stand here forever, noble or not."

Davy clamored at them. "Are you coming back, Daddy? Mommy, I want him to come back!"

"Oh, yes, Davy," she said. "He's coming back. There's no keeping him from it, I can see."

She smiled at Sean and saw tears fill his eyes. "Why, Sean," she said. "Darling, don't"—she found her handkerchief—"Here."

"Kiss me," he whispered.

It was not easy, what with Davy hugging his left leg and trying to climb into his arms, but they managed a long kiss. "That's good," he said. He glanced at his wristwatch. "Oh God, I've got to go, or the fine job will be lost to me! Davy, I brought you a present. Ah, we'll open it together in the morning."

He was gone.

"He's coming back," Davy said happily. "I can tell he's coming back. He didn't say goodbye or anything."

Cynthia wiped the tears of laughter and rue from her eyes. "He meant to come back before he got here," she said. "I wouldn't put anything beyond him. And it was his luck that Mimi and that wretched puppy helped him—his Irish luck. It's been lonely, I'll admit . . . I know how Mimi feels, in a way. It'll be the gay old life over again. No better, no worse, I daresay —but it'll be life, anyway."

She sat down and smoothed back her hair.

Davy did not hear her. He had walked to the door and now he picked

34

up something from the floor. It was the rag puppy. He held it between his thumb and finger.

"I don't want this old thing anymore," he said.

He came to her and deposited it in her lap.

"Goodnight," she said. "We'll see you in the morning—Daddy and me."

He stood above her, his eyes grave. She thought, that's how he'll look when he's fifteen. "Shall I come and tuck you in?" she asked.

He shook his head. "No, thanks. I can do it myself."

He marched to the door and turned to look back at her.

"Merry Christmas to you," he said, so formally that she could have laughed again, if tears had not come back to her eyes instead.

"Merry Christmas to us all," she replied.

He nodded and went upstairs alone for the first time in his life. She sat there on the sofa, holding the rag puppy on her lap and waiting to hear him open the windows. Or would he call for her to come and help him? She listened . . . No, he was doing without her. Then she heard Mimi. The dog was whining again, whimpering and sniffing, searching for the rag puppy.

"Here," Cynthia said, tossing the toy to her. "You may have it, since nobody wants it now."

She watched while the poodle lifted the rag puppy tenderly between her teeth and carried it to the corner.

"It's all you have, poor thing," Cynthia said aloud, "and I suppose I'll have to do something about that, too, sometime."

As if in answer, Mimi gave one short, sharp bark and curling herself around the puppy, she went to sleep.

Sitting there on the couch, Cynthia took up her knitting. Happy, that was the word. She was simply happy. She hadn't felt happiness for weeks. She had tried to make anger serve, and she had used industry, but there was no substitute for the happiness of love. She glanced up at the tree, blazing with lights. Those lights—ought she not to turn them off? The electricity bill—no, she'd not be thrifty tonight! Cost what it might, now and for all time to come, let the Christmas lights be shining when Sean came home.

35

Christmas
Away
from Home

What makes a Christmas? *Home* is the first word that springs into my mind, and home was what I did not have that strange faraway year. One day I had a house, a family, a garden, neighbors. A quiet old-fashioned Chinese city spread around me, and over the city wall, thousands of years old, a hundred feet high and broad enough to drive four automobiles abreast if there had been any such vehicles in the city, which there weren't, a great mountain lifted its head. You would have said that no life could be so stable as mine, no home so secure, no friends so true.

And then one morning, it was all no more. The war which had crept down the river so mildly, so seemingly kind, to set up good government in place of the greed of local warlords, this war turned suddenly vicious. The leaders changed, the slogans were written anew overnight. Instead of "Rescue the people," the cry was "Kill the foreigners," and we were foreigners, because we were white people.

On a windy, cold morning, soon after sunrise, war drove us out of the comfortable house, out of our home, and we stood bleak and alone in the dead garden, where frost had killed all the flowers and the grass was brown. White men already lay murdered in the streets.

I reckoned without friends. Chinese friends came from beyond the gates, from the college where I taught, from the shops where we bought food and fuel, from the neighborhood, and by these friends we were saved and hidden until rescue came.

We were rescued, we were taken to Shanghai, and from that crowded and panic-stricken city we chose to go to Japan. The months passed, the war subsided, peace was patched up, and we came back again to a Shang-

38

hai subdued and apathetic. But the house up the river in the walled city was home no more, that dream-haunted house, where my father had lived with me for ten years after my mother's death, where my children had spent their first wonder-filled Christmas days, where men and women of my own land, lonely away from home, had found a sort of home, and where Chinese friends had come to see what Christmas meant. The war, or so it seemed to me, had destroyed Christmas too.

So we spent Christmas huddled with two other American refugee families in a rented house in Shanghai. Shanghai is not a good city in which to spend Christmas. There are too many people there who do not know what Christmas is about.

Christmas? It seemed impossible and best forgotten, if one could forget the Christmas dawn, when the Chinese college students, in the delicacy of their courtesy, came to sing carols under our windows.

That Christmas in Shanghai we knew there would be no young voices under the windows of the rented house. And there would be no Christmas gifts wrapped in Chinese red paper, given by Chinese friends to console us for not being in our own country on our great feast day, no packages of sesame toffee and larded cakes and barley sticks.

But stop—we had children in the rented house, three families of us had children, and of course where there are children there must be Christmas. We were all desperately poor that year; we were always poor, but that year I say it was desperate, for war had stripped us of everything. Yet we scraped together a few Chinese dollars and we bargained for a fat hen to roast, we found ingredients for a plum pudding of sorts, and we bought some Chinese sweets. Then we three American mothers, pooling our little resources of scraps and bits, shaped dolls and stuffed animals; we made picture books, bright pictures cut from magazines and the text, the verses and stories we wrote for such happy illustration. Somehow or other there were tiny gifts for each other, too.

I cannot say it was much of a Christmas, and yet it was. We even found a little holly somewhere, I remember, and we put it over the mantel, in the small living room we shared, although each in our own homes had been used to great bundles of holly at Christmastime, brought to us by a farmer outside the city, who cut the wild holly on the mountain and

40

carried it into the city in two loads swung over a carrying pole. But the solitary branch of holly was precious, for the children's sake.

The children were happy with what they had, but it was I who was not happy. I was angry to the bottom of my soul, not angry at anybody in the house, but furious at fate.

Then the wonderful thing happened. I sold a story. Months before, I had sent it away on the long journey to America and the very day after Christmas a small, a very small check reached me. I tore open the letter, I remember, and out fell the precious slip of paper. I had a quick moment of sorrow that the check had not come before Christmas, for I could have bought something more for everybody. Then, and how strange that I am not ashamed, I was glad. Yesterday had not been really Christmas. It had been a day of sad remembering, of weariness at the doubtful future.

Very well, said I in my wickedness, I would do what I had never done before in my life, and what I have never done since. I would take this bit of paper to the bank, I would cash it into solid silver money, and I would spend it all at once.

So, quite alone, and altogether selfishly, I went into the Chinese city and bought a small beautiful bowl, a clear white, I remember, embossed with a spare branch of budded plum blossoms. It was very breakable and foolish indeed, in those days when bread and not beauty was the concern. Then I bought a piece of silk, about six feet long, heavy hand-woven Chinese silk of a soft blue. That was a scarf. At a pinch, I could make it serve with my old suit as a blouse. I could twist it about my head as a tight little hat. I could simply hang it on the wall and look at it, so beautiful it was. And all the time I was buying these selfish gifts, I saved enough for a book. What book? An anthology, of course, which would be stuffed with memories of books I had owned before and which were now gone. And so I bought an anthology of English essays.

This was my Christmas. I took my secret back to the rented house where nobody noticed anything anyway, and I set the bowl high on a little shelf across the room from my bed. I kept the blue hand-woven silk always in sight, and the book, ah, the book, I read again and again, and blessed be the memories of the mind.

By all the laws of decency I ought to feel shame, I suppose, but I never

41

have. I really understood at last that man does not live by bread alone, and if not man, then certainly not woman.

Christmas it was, a strange kind of Christmas, and I have never had another like it, because I have not needed it. But there it was, and in a way, it was the best of Christmases, because it was the beginning from which much came.

The New
Christmas

Mary Barnatt closed her checkbook and looked at the balance she had just written on what she called her scribble paper. She could never believe the bank made proper additions, although the subtractions were always painfully correct and the balances were always impossibly small. Today, however, with Christmas shining over the edge of the horizon, she had to face the fact that the balance was impossibly small. Five children and Adam, her husband and their father! She was sometimes, even often, embarrassed these days, to answer a stranger's question:

"How many children have you?"

"Five—two girls and three boys."

"Five!" The stranger's exclamation was either reproach or pity.

Yet she could not think of which child she could have done without, if she had thought of it in time. They were all so welcome, so—necessary. What would she do without thirteen-year-old Ruth, or twelve-year-old Brooke or ten-year-old Penny and the two little boys, Jimmy and Jack? Were they all planned for? Yes and no. That is, she and Adam had certainly not said, two—or three—or even four, and no more. And now—well, now in spite of all this talk of overpopulation, they still thought it was no one's business how many children they should have. It was only these times when she had to face the bank balance that she said to herself, "Well, at least I'm not pregnant again!"

Adam had been doing so well in his job as a junior executive in a big oil industry. He had risen amazingly fast. But this year, only a few days ago, indeed, he had said to her:

"Go easy on presents this Christmas, honey! My job looks steady,

44

but some companies are letting fellows like me go."

It was the first time she had ever heard caution from him, and at this moment she remembered it very soberly indeed. She had such confidence in his brilliance, his talents, his reliability, that she could not believe that any company could spare him. On the other hand—

She sighed and put the checkbook safely away, the alarming balance tucked into it so that she must face it whenever she wrote a check.

Nor did she say a word to Adam about it when he came home late for dinner, as he too often did these days. He earned the living of all of them and it was her business to make do with what he gave her, which was always everything. She ran the evening smoothly as usual. After dinner Adam took from the book table in the living room a technical trade magazine and stretched his tall frame on the adjustable green velvet chair she had given him last Christmas.

"Gosh, I look forward to this chair every evening," he exclaimed as he sank into it.

She moved the light so that it shone on his page and, kissing his cheek, she tripped into the utility room to finish her ironing while the children gathered around the kitchen table to do their homework, except for the little boys who had crayons and color books.

Standing there at the ironing board, as she had to do at least twice a week, she thought, troubled, of how she could manage a Christmas for these blessed children of hers. Were they old enough to understand— even Ruth, who only the other day had said something about a new coat —one with a fur collar perhaps? Life had been easy for them, as it was for most American children, and while she herself had never been one to care about hypothetical Joneses, she liked her children to be as well dressed as any in this neighborhood where they had lived now for as many years as the children could remember. Perhaps life *had* been too easy for them. Perhaps they were not mature enough to understand the exigencies and fluctuations of their father's business. Perhaps even she did not understand fully enough the responsibility that Adam carried! But how could one compel children to maturity? Didn't they have to grow into it as their bodies grow? Didn't they—

Here her thoughts were broken off abruptly. She heard an argument

46

from the kitchen and set down her iron and listened. Ruth was saying something, her clear young voice very decided.

"I tell you, I left my purse on the kitchen windowsill when I came home from school today!"

"Then you shouldn't have." That was Penny's silvery little voice.

"You never put your things away like Mother tells you." That was big brother, Brooke.

"Shut up, Brooke," Ruth said rudely.

Mary Barnatt, mother, took a step toward the kitchen and then stayed her steps. No, this was their business. It was true that Ruth had a naughty way of leaving her purse anywhere when she came in, too often on the kitchen windowsill.

"You took it, Jimmy!" Ruth was saying.

"I did not!" Jimmy was the hot-tempered one.

"And I didn't," Jack said, abstracted. He was the busy one, the detached artist, who lived his own life. "And," he continued musingly, "I s'all make my elephunt pink."

"There's no such thing as a pink elephant," Ruth said irritably.

"I don't care is or isn't," Jack said. "Mine is pink, 'cause that is how I make it."

"And I say," Ruth declared, "that not one of you may leave this table until he or she tells me where my purse is. It has my five dollars in it that Grandmother sent me last week for my birthday—well, almost five. I spent ten cents for a little cherry tart at school lunch today and I didn't eat it."

"Where is the tart?" Jimmy asked with sudden interest.

"In the refrigerator," Ruth said. "I'm eating it before I go to bed. So where is my purse?"

The silence was long—too long for young endurance. Ruth broke it.

"All right, you kids! I'll give my cherry tart to the one who finds my purse."

There was a general scramble of departing feet, running through the house at top speed. Mary took up her iron and smiled. Wise Ruth! But she had not finished the cuff of the shirt before Jimmy's voice rang out.

"I found it—I found it! Guess where! Under the radiator in the living room!"

47

"Give it to me," Ruth said. "I'll see if the change is all there."

She opened the purse, apparently, for silence fell. All the children were back, waiting.

"The four dollars are here," Ruth said, "but there's no change."

Penny's clear little voice explained. "Now I know why Jimmy's tin can of money is so full."

"Oh, all right," Jimmy grumbled. "I'll go and get it, meany!"

Again Mary the mother stepped toward the kitchen door to intervene. Jimmy taking change from a purse—any purse! Again she stopped herself. Let her see how mature they were!

There was silence. Ruth was counting the change. "It's all here," she announced.

"Now I get the cherry tart," Jimmy said joyfully.

"I don't think you should," Brooke's voice was firm. "You stole money. That's not right."

"It's bad," Penny agreed.

"Now my elephunt is all pink," Jack said dreamily.

Ruth said nothing. Mary the mother waited. No, she would not interfere. There was thinking going on and thinking meant growing.

"Still," Ruth's voice was thoughtful. "I ought to do what I said I would. What Jimmy does is *his* business. What I do is *my* business. And he did bring back my purse and all the change. And I should have put my purse away in the first place."

There was silence. Mary the mother heard the refrigerator door open and shut.

"Here's the cherry tart," Ruth said.

"Thank you, Ruthie, but—" Jimmy began and broke off. Then there was silence again, very brief. "I guess—"

He faltered. Cherry tart was his favorite food. He went on bravely. "I guess I ought to give everybody a bite—like a punishment for me because I did take the little money out of the purse and put it in my tin can."

This was evidently done, for Jimmy's voice, after a brief silence, was doleful. "Anyway some is left," he announced.

"Most of it is left," Ruth said. "They all took tiny bites—and I won't take any, because I gave it all to you."

48

"It's a extra good cherry tart," Jimmy said amiably.

Mary entered upon the scene, smiling. "So," she said cheerfully. "Now it's my turn. Not for cherry tart—oh, no, I can see that's all gone, Jimmy —but I've listened and I'm proud of you all. I think you're ready for an idea I have for us—every one of us. I haven't been sure until now. But you've been so—so wise in this affair of the cherry tart that I'm going to ask that you think about a new kind of Christmas."

And then she sat down at the head of the table and simply she told them that there wasn't much money this year. Life was like that—changing all the time, good one year, then not so good maybe. Yet Christmas was always the same. With or without money, it came about, year after year.

"Let's think what Christmas really means to each of you. Jack, now that your elephant is all pink to the very end of its little tail, we'll begin with you. What is Christmas?"

"Santy Claus," Jack said. He was crayoning green grass under his pink elephant.

"Silly," Jimmy said. "Santa Claus is only a story man. *I* think Christmas means presents."

"A tree, with bright lights," Penny said.

"Fun," Brooke said. "No school and turkey and plum pudding. New books and games, too, I guess."

"A birthday," Ruth said. "The birthday of Jesus, and lovely Christmas music and holly in the house and all of us together all day. And Christmas parties—something new to wear—like a coat—" She paused, smiling. "With a fur collar, maybe?"

"All of you are thinking of the Christmases you've always had," Mary the mother said. "How could we make another kind of Christmas, something entirely new? Oh, of course we'll give each other presents—I'm not sure about the coat with a fur collar, Ruthie—this year, at least—but maybe. We'll see. But you've all been thinking of what you'll do—and get. I'd like you to think of a gift you give—that doesn't cost money, but is something of yourself. That's what Jesus Christ gave—Himself. He seems never to have had any money. He just had His youth, His strength, His concern for other people, all people really, although perhaps He tried to

49

help the helpless ones first. What, for example, would He do if He lived here in our town?"

They looked at one another. They looked at her, faces thoughtful, minds working hard to grasp the inner meaning of what she had said. Outside the kitchen window snow was beginning to fall. It had been predicted, this snow, upon a wave of cold air from the northwest.

"Like me shoveling the snow from old Mrs. Thomson's walk in the mornings?" Brooke said.

"You'd have to get up earlier for school," Ruth said.

"And you like to sleep, Brooke—you know you do," Penny added.

"Maybe he wouldn't have to do it every time it snows—just at Christmas," Jimmy suggested.

"What's the good of that?" Ruth asked. "If you do something as a gift, then you have to really keep your word."

"Right," Mary the mother said. "Like promising a cherry tart!"

Brooke laughed. "Okay—that's my Christmas gift! I'll begin tomorrow. Shall I tell Mrs. Thomson?"

"Last year we sent her a potted poinsettia. I think she'll like this year's Christmas gift better," Mary said. "I would, if I were her age."

"I'll iron my own clothes from now on—forever," Ruth said suddenly.

"That's *my* gift from you," Mary said. "Thank you, darling." It had been a matter between them. Ruth was old enough but too often forgetful, too often moody, too often late.

"I won't hide my shoes and things under the living room big chair—or somewhere—" Jimmy said. "I'll put them away, so I won't forget where they are, so everybody doesn't have to look for them."

"Thank *you,* Jimmy," his mother said. "That will be a great help to all of us."

"I will help Mrs. Jackson with her baby until her burned hand is all well," Penny said. Mrs. Jackson was a neighbor with a baby just learning to walk and into everything, as she put it.

"That's a real Christmas present," Mary the mother said.

"And I," Jack said, "I think I will always—always—always—do what Daddy tells me to do and I always forget—like feeding the dog and putting water in his bowl."

50

"*That* will please Daddy," Mary said. She went on gently. "Now you have the idea, all of you, and you see what you can do with it. You'll want to give presents to other people—so think what you can give of *yourself*. Of course sometimes you'll need money to buy what you want. Then you can earn it by giving your own time and strength in work."

"Or," Ruth said, "I can use what Grandmother gave me to buy new slippers for Dad—have you *seen* those slippers he wears, Mother? How can he *keep* them on his *feet!* I *was* going to buy a silver bracelet for myself—not real silver, I guess—"

"That's giving yourself by denying yourself," Mary said. "There are so many ways to give of yourself. It makes the gift more pleasure to give as well as to get."

They were all silent for a moment. She watched their thoughtful faces. A new truth was becoming a part of them, a new dimension had been added to their lives, a new seed planted in the garden of their souls. They were far more ready for it than she had imagined. She had done them an injustice. To keep a child a child too long was a wrong done to that child. She had a gift to give them, too. She must share the privilege of responsibility with them from now on.

In the silence Adam came into the kitchen. "Where is everybody?" he demanded. "The house is so quiet I went to sleep."

"You looked tired and I'm glad you slept," Mary said.

And then quite simply she explained to him the new Christmas giving. "New for us," she said, "but really as old as the Christmas story itself."

He listened, his face grave. "Good," he said firmly, "but I have a warning. Don't give a gift and then take it back again."

"What do you mean by that, Dad?" Brooke asked. For a moment he looked younger than twelve.

"If you say you give of yourself, you must keep your word or it's taking back your gift. You, for example, clearing the snow from old Mrs. Thomson's walk. If you forget, or think of something else, and don't clear the snow away that morning, you've taken back the good gift."

"I see what you mean," Brooke said soberly.

"Well," Adam the father said, "I see I'll have to do some thinking for myself. What shall *I* give? You are all ahead of me."

51

"I haven't thought of *my* gifts, either," Mary the mother said. "You and I will have to do some thinking together."

She rose as she spoke. "Come on, darling—let's go and think together."

And they went away, hand-in-hand.

"They're so wonderful, children are," she said. "They understood exactly what I meant. I had only to point it out—what real giving means."

"And I had only to affirm it by showing the necessity of honoring your word," he said.

"Ruth knows that, too," she maintained, and she told him the story of the cherry tart.

"She'd promised," Mary said, "and so she kept her word. However wrong Jimmy had been, she was right. I'll never belittle again a child's understanding."

"Perhaps that's *your* gift, Mary mine," he said.

The Christmas Child

"If the baby is a boy," she said passionately, "I'll just—die!"

"You won't die, my dear," Dr. West said briskly. "You're too strong. Besides, it's wicked to talk like that, especially on Christmas Eve. Suppose Mary had said such a thing to Joseph nearly two thousand years ago!"

Sue Wayne turned her head restlessly on the pillow. "There wasn't a war on then and she wasn't alone, as I am, with Ron thousands of miles away in some jungle in Vietnam! Where's Vietnam, anyway? Who ever heard of such a place before we started sending our men there? Four months and three days after our wedding and Ron was gone! I'm so lonely!"

"That other young mother long ago was very much alone, too," Dr. West said, "and there was a sort of war, there always is." He was washing his hands and drying them energetically, as he did everything, though his hair was white. He had retired two years before and then had begun practice again when Ronald Storne, his junior partner, had been called for military service. He kept on talking now as he busied himself. "Not only alone, was Mary, but she had a strange secret which she kept to herself, for how could Joseph understand what had happened to her when she couldn't understand it herself? She must have had her forebodings, too, for she knew she would bear a son so extraordinary that he was doomed to be persecuted, despised, rejected of men. I daresay the shadow of the cross fell early on her heart. Get up now, Sue, and begin to march again."

"Oh, *leave* me alone!" she cried.

He came to the side of the narrow hospital bed and stood there, a small, blunt-nosed man with a clipped white moustache on his upper lip.

54

"Get up," he ordered.

She looked at him, her blue eyes angry, and turned her head away. "If it's a boy, I can't go through with it. Wars never end. You're right. If it's not Vietnam it will be somewhere else. He'll go off as Ron has—it happens over and over again. I wish I'd never married. What the hell! I had a good job. No, I went and fell in love! See where it's got me!"

"Sue!" Dr. West's voice was stern. "Don't belittle love! I won't have it —especially where Ron is concerned. You and Ron love each other. Honor that love now when you are bearing his child. Honor him by doing your part bravely."

A great sob tore itself from her breast, and suddenly she wailed.

"I miss him so—he can't even be with me when our baby is born!"

"No, he can't," Doctor West agreed. "He's doing what he must—he's doing his duty. Come on now—do yours!"

He lifted her from the bed, surprisingly strong for his age, and set her on her feet. She was a small woman, brown haired and with blue eyes proclaiming an Irish ancestry.

"I won't!" she insisted stubbornly.

Dr. West caught the flash from those blue eyes. "You've had that temper since I first told you to stick out your tongue. You were three years old and you were coming down with chicken pox. Now march."

"I still won't," she said, but sparks of laughter glinted in her eyes.

"Come *on,*" Dr. West said. "I'll march, too."

"No," she said, biting her lip.

But she did, as she knew she would. For if she didn't, wouldn't he perhaps tell Ron that she'd behaved badly? The two doctors, one so old, the other so young, made fun together of her tempers and wilfullness.

"You're my darling spoiled brat!" Ronnie would say, his dark eyes brimming with love and laughter.

Thinking of those eyes, her own now filled with tears. She paused in the march, and turning to the short stocky doctor marching at her side, she put her head on his shoulder and sobbed. He patted her back.

"There now—a woman doesn't cry because she's having a baby!"

"I'll cry if I want to, and I can't keep from thinking that—that he won't

56

stay a baby,'' she sobbed. ''He'll grow up and be a man and he'll go off, too, to some Vietnam or other and be blown to pieces and all this will be of no use. My life will be wasted—all the trouble—''

''The love won't be wasted,'' he said patiently. ''Love can't be wasted. It always counts, throughout life—yours and Ronnie's and his.''

She lifted her head and for an instant looked into his unwavering eyes. Then pain seized her.

''Let's get on with this,'' she said shortly and she began again to march.

Far away on the other side of the world Ronald Storne was operating on a makeshift table set up in a farmhouse in a village where the battle had only that day taken place. Christmas Eve! Last year he and Sue had spent their first Christmas together in their own house. Even before he had met her he had wanted to buy that house, the home of his dreams. He used to pass it every day on his way to school, for his father's farm, where he grew up, was outside the town. Every day he passed it twice, going and coming, and he often paused to look at the house, then deserted, and to wonder who had lived there long ago, and how they could have left it, and why. When he and Sue were engaged he had taken her there on their very first weekend.

''That's our home,'' he had told her.

She had stared at it in silence. Then she said, ''But won't it cost a fortune to make it livable?''

''Bit by bit we'll do it, and I intend to begin it now.''

They had spent the day there, and finding a door unlocked, they had gone from room to room. Then he had summed it up.

''Good pine floors upstairs, good oak floors downstairs, a big cellar, a big attic, eight rooms, a well under that old pump—we could live here right away, Sue, as soon as we're married, if you don't mind living the way the people who built the house did, just for a while, of course.''

''I don't mind,'' Sue had said.

That was Sue, he thought tenderly, his hands busy. Here in this hell of a place, the thought of the house gave him courage. How cool it always was under their big sycamore tree in the front yard and how cool, how blessedly cold it was in winter when snow piled against the front door! The

57

house was built of fieldstone and once, in more peaceful times, it had been the century-old farmhouse of sturdy English settlers. His ancestors had been English, too—Quakers originally, under William Penn, but somewhere along the way their faith had declined until it was now only part of his family's history. What, he asked himself, would renew that faith today or ever could?

Then he thought of Sue. How bravely she had lived in the house, how joyously! They had spent their honeymoon there, working together on one room and another, though there still was no heat in it except the big fireplaces, and no light except for kerosene lamps. But they had laughed over everything and never once had she complained.

"Brave little wife," he had told her.

"*Your* wife," she had whispered, in his arms.

Ah, that was his faith now, his faith in love and life! If only he could see the end of this present horror! When, oh when, would people learn to love instead of hate?

The question hovered in his mind, unanswered, indeed scarcely asked, in the crowded, endless hours on the edge of a battlefield, now here, now there, as the enemy led. It was difficult, too, even to think of the enemy. These small brown men and women all looked alike to him, each a suffering human frame, destroyed by wounds, dying if he could not save them quickly enough. He was a surgeon and, he liked to think, a skilled one. Just now he was amputating a leg below the thigh, a thin wiry brown leg, the skin as tough as leather. He glanced at the drugged face, a young man, a man no older than himself, a peasant, this morning tilling his fields—Christmas Eve, but here the weather was mild enough to sow one field and reap another in continuous planting and harvests. A wonderful country, he often thought, if it were not devastated by unending war, a country whose people were kind and good, people of courage and energy, like the people in the town near which he had grown up and in which Sue had lived all her life. He thought of his little Sue—he was always thinking of her, for about now the baby was due, and she wanted a girl. Well, let it be a girl! Maybe women some day would be able to stop these wars. But maybe not. Certainly not in his generation! He tied an artery carefully and the man groaned.

58

"A touch more of the anesthetic," he ordered the nurse, "but watch the pulse."

The stolid middle-aged woman obeyed. Though she was off duty for a few hours, she had volunteered this morning, when he was sent to the village. He stopped thinking about Sue and concentrated on his work. At least he was not responsible for death. At least his part in this beastly war was saving life, not destroying it!

"There," he said at last. "I've done my best. He'll pull through, I think."

"I think not," the nurse said. "His heart has just stopped."

She spoke with dreadful calm, as though she did not care. But he knew she did care. They had worked side by side day after day, without really getting to know each other, absorbed in their life-saving work. Besides, it was true. It was too late—the man had lost too much blood. He was dead.

He turned his back while the man was taken away, and though his lips trembled, he washed his hands with fierce energy.

"Next case," he said abruptly over his shoulder.

But what, Sue was thinking, was the use of this pain, this agony of birth, endured by women generation after generation, if people kept on killing each other, generation after generation? She was only one of many women at this very moment, on this Christmas Eve, their men far away. And were they all thinking these same thoughts? This profound loneliness, this struggle of her body to give birth to a new life—ah, she was not the only one!

"Help me," she moaned.

"I am helping you all I can," the doctor said. "But I can only help you as you help yourself."

That was the loneliness—she had to do it herself. It was woman's work, wasteful as it seemed, wasteful of her strength, her energy, her own faith. Faith in what? For her at this moment, only her faith in Ron, his faith in her. Even if Ron were here she would still have to do it herself. It was her task—a woman's task, the fulfillment of a duty, an obligation, which she had begun that evening two years ago when she had first let Ron kiss her . . .

Or perhaps it had begun the moment she first saw him, which had been on another Christmas Eve, a silly beautiful moment when they had turned a corner on a street, she from the east, he from the west, so that they collided, each with arms full of packages, and she was knocked breathless. He had dropped his packages to help her pick up hers and she began picking up his, so that they had been obliged, laughing, to stop in a handy drugstore and sort themselves out.

"And since we are here," Ron had said, "we might as well have coffee and a sandwich. I'm hungry."

"So am I," she had said, which was true, for she had been belated in her Christmas shopping and had skipped lunch entirely.

Their packages were heaped together on a chair and while they sorted them out, they were talking as though they had already known each other.

"Careful," she said. "That's a china pussycat for my great aunt Sue, the one I'm named after. She loves cats—"

"So your name is Sue—" he had said.

"What's yours?" she asked.

That was the way it began. It went on to their showing each other the gifts they had bought and describing the people for whom they were bought.

"My father is a teacher in the high school," she said, "and so I bought him a book. He never has enough books. It's a new kind of dictionary. Want to see?"

She had unwrapped it and it was indeed a good dictionary—he, too, had bought it last year in his final months of internship. She was talking and unwrapping.

"And my mother likes jewelry—she hasn't very much, but now that I'm earning my own money—I'm a secretary—I bought her this pearl pin."

"No brothers or sisters?" he had asked.

"No, I'm the only one," she said. "And I'm spoiled," she added in a funny little matter-of-fact way. "Everyone says so and it's true."

He had laughed. "How are you spoiled?" he had demanded.

"You'll find out—if we get to know each other," she had said. And then, suddenly changing, she demanded to know what he had bought.

"I have two sisters—much younger—and my parents. I've bought my father some tools he's been wanting—and a scarf for my mother."

"Don't unwrap them," she said. "Or just the scarf—oh, it's pretty! I love green."

"Charm bracelets for the girls," he said, showing her the pretty silver toys.

And all the time they were munching their sandwiches and drinking coffee. When the moment came to part, they had looked at each other and were suddenly silent for a moment. Then Ron spoke.

"See here," he said. "I've known you always. This is no accident. The moment when we turned that corner at the same time—that moment—someone, somewhere, planned it. I know it."

She had gazed up at him, he so much the taller. "Do you believe that, really?" she asked.

"I believe in life," he said. "And when a door opens which promises more life, I hold the door open until I can enter."

A mystic joy swept them both. Outside from somewhere there came the sound of Christmas music. It had been playing all along but until now they had not heard it. Now they heard it in a glorious burst of music. "Joy to the world—"

"That's our music," Ron said, his gaze steadfast upon her upturned face.

She had laughed for pure joy. "Since you know all about my family," she said, "you had better come around tomorrow and see how they like their presents. We live at—"

"Now then," Dr. West said. "We're getting somewhere. You've been marching like a good trooper. The pains are coming closer together."

"How do you know, pray tell," she said, laughing. "They're *my* pains —not yours!"

"You've been telling me, smiling about something and then screwing up your pretty face!"

"You've been wonderful to stay by me," she moaned. Suddenly the pain was bad again, very bad—oh, this was the worst yet, this pain dragging at her very entrails! "I thought nurses—stayed by—it's good of you to— yourself—" she gave up trying to talk, and panting, she leaned upon his shoulder and bit her lips.

61

"I promised Ron I'd stay with you myself," he said gruffly. "There—there—I think you had better get ready. I'll call the nurse now. But I'm here, just the same—"

She lay down and closed her eyes. The pain was edging off but she must prepare herself for the next great surge of agony. So Ron was thinking of her—thinking of this very moment when she was alone. For she was always alone without him. But he had made Dr. West promise . . .

And what a wonderful Christmas that had been when she and Ron had met—their first Christmas, really—because both of them had known immediately that they were in love—the very next morning when she flew to open the front door as soon as he rang the bell. She had known it was he, for who else would come on a Christmas morning and who else would actually leave his parents and his sisters?

"I told them I'd met a girl," he told her afterwards. "And I told them it was the girl I was going to marry. So they let me come—"

Here she paused to face the pain again. Oh, it was very bad now—and coming so close—no time to catch her breath. She held out her hands blindly.

"Help me," she cried.

She felt her hand caught in other hands, the doctor—the nurse. Sweat ran down her face.

"I'm going to give you something soon—very soon—" Doctor West said. "But if you can just make a couple more good hard pushes—"

"Of course," she muttered. "Of course—"

In the blessed painless moment she drifted off again, escaping to Ron . . .

He had stayed for hours that first Christmas Day. He had stayed until dinnertime. Then reluctantly he had got up to go home, for that he had promised.

"I promised the family I'd be back," he told her.

"So you should," she said.

It did not matter what they said. They knew they must be together.

"Do come again," her mother told him.

"Any time," her father added.

They liked Ron. But if they hadn't it wouldn't have mattered. She'd

62

simply have picked up her coat and followed him, left everything, every-body, behind—forever, if it had been necessary—only it wasn't, because he came back the very next day.

She was interrupted by pain, snatching her out of the past, forcing her into the present. Now all her mind—and heart—and body—must concentrate—upon this fulfillment—of love—

"I shall give you a hypo," Dr. West said.

She shook her head. "I don't want it," she gasped. "I want to—do everything—myself!"

He stared at her, hypodermic in hand. "You don't *want* help?" he said almost stupidly.

She shook her head and closed her eyes and held back a scream. Then she drifted off again . . .

And there had been no use in delaying the wedding when they knew perfectly sure—they had not bothered even to talk much about who they were or what had been their lives before they met—all that no longer mattered. Whatever their past lives had been would not have mattered—unimportant detail, preparing them for each other.

"Only if we had not been what we are," Ron had explained while they were skiing together, "we wouldn't have recognized each other."

That was the day after Christmas, and every day afterwards they were together—he, in the evenings, of course, after his holiday was over. He'd had only three days. And she worked resolutely hard at her job because the days were too long while she waited for evening.

Dr. West broke in. "My dear, there is no use in torturing yourself—"

"Not—torturing—" she panted.

She dissolved into pain. Her hospital jacket was drenched with sweat. She felt herself dizzy, unthinking, absorbed into a monstrous wave of agony out of which Ron's face emerged—Ron's face when he said, that night by the fire, she and he sitting there alone, tired by the skiing and so happy, her parents thoughtfully absent.

"How shall I ask you to marry me? I've thought of a hundred ways—it's too soon, you may say, but it was not too soon even the moment I saw you. I'd often wondered how I would ask the girl I—and where I would meet you—and now that we've met, all the ways are—silly—and too slow.

63

I simply love you. I simply want to marry you."

They were in each other's arms. There was nothing more to be said. They knew.

"But are you sure—so soon, darling?" her mother had asked the next day.

"Sure, I'm sure," she had answered flippantly because she was too madly happy.

She wanted to be married on St. Valentine's Day, idiot that she was, but he said soberly that he wanted to get his partnership first with an older doctor, and his own offices, and so they had waited until the next Christmas Eve—a year, endlessly long—but so happy—so happy—and every weekend they worked on the house.

She was moaning aloud now and she felt her hand strongly grasped. It was Dr. West again.

"You're doing beautifully—and bravely—I shall write Ron all about this —he'll be proud of you—very proud."

"He'd better be," she gasped with a crooked smile.

But of course they had gone that very first afternoon to see his family and she was so glad, so very glad they had, for his parents had moved the next year to Florida, because his mother had rheumatism badly and needed a warm climate. A wonderful family, she thought, but still it had been nice having Ron to herself after they were married. Such a lovely, happy wedding, Ron so handsome, but the girls were handsome, too, though not so tall as he, of course—and after the wedding they had gone straight to the lovely old house, waiting for them to bring it back to life again—and Ron had thrown open the ancient Dutch door in front of the house and had lifted her over the threshold—and together they took possession of their home.

And that night, in front of their first blazing fire in the big cavernous fireplace in the living room, she, in his arms in the armchair that was a wedding present from his family, had asked a question.

"When shall we have a baby?" she had asked.

"I want you to myself for a whole year," Ron had said.

But they had not waited a year, after all. In the spring—in the spring, loving each so much—so much—

64

"Now then," Dr. West said. "This is the moment. Bear down, Sue—that's a brave little—mother—ah, here he is—right on time—now, my dear, rejoice—rejoice that a son is born!"

She began to laugh, she could not keep from laughing, a deep, half-crying laughter. So this was what had come of that night in spring, that night when she and Ron had looked at each other in the dimly lighted room, their bedroom! She had plucked a question from her breast, another question that night.

"Why should we wait?" she had whispered.

"Are you ready for the child?" he had asked.

"I am ready," she had answered.

Ah, of course one couldn't be sure—only they were sure—and she had not been surprised in Dr. West's office, two months later.

"You will have a Christmas baby," he had announced.

"Let me see him," she said now.

The doctor lifted a blanket-wrapped bundle so that she could see him and she looked into a round cheerful small face. Yes, he was cheerful, small as he was. She laughed.

"He looks so—self-satisfied," she said.

"He ought to look so," Dr. West declared. "He has nice parents. I promised Ron I'd take a snapshot of his son before he was an hour old. I have the camera all ready. Here—let him rest in the crook of your arm —mother and child."

He put the baby gently beside her, and she looked down into the miracle of the little face. Dr. West gazed at them, and his old eyes filled with sentimental tears.

"Now smile," he ordered.

And she smiled.

Far away, days later, Ron paused for a brief rest between operations. It was mid-winter, but winter never touched this torrid land. The moist wind was heavy with the fetid odors of blood and death. He threw himself into a bamboo chair and closed his eyes. Then he heard a voice.

"I don't want to disturb you, doctor," the nurse said. "But I saw a letter for you—I think it's—"

65

He opened his eyes and seized the letter and tore open the envelope. A photograph fell out, a picture in color. Bless old West, it was of Sue and—

He gazed into that small face so near hers. So that was he, that was his son! He turned the picture over and read the old doctor's scrawled handwriting on the back.

"I wonder if long ago Mary knew that a savior had been born from her womb, a great man who could lead the world to peace, if men would follow him? Anyway, she hoped, as all mothers hope! Who knows? I keep hoping, too, with every baby I deliver. Who knows, I ask? Perhaps it is your son and Sue's, who will be the one to find the way."

No Room
at the Inn

Over the horizon I see the glow of Christmas coming, the Christmas of this year of Our Lord, one thousand nine hundred and fifty. All the Christmas times of my life are reflected in that glow, for each Christmas is part of all that have gone before and to tradition and memory in every family, the new Christmas adds its part. Take in our family, the Big Party.

The day before Christmas Eve now in our house is always the day of the Big Party, the first event for us of Christmas week. It has become our tradition. Yet actually the Big Party began decades ago and halfway around the world, when I was a little girl. We lived in the Chinese countryside in a plain little gray brick house. Whatever luxury we had was not in the house but in the landscape of lush valleys and distant purple mountains. Christmas was joyful but simple in that house, for there was never much money. But every year there was one golden gorgeous glorious event when I saw plenty of everything, toys and delicious foods in lavishly beautiful rooms. Once a year during Christmas week a kindly English lady, the wife of an official in the British Customs, gave all the Western children a Christmas party. Her house was the usual enormous and stately pile of brick with which the British Empire in those days maintained its dignity in Asia. The house stood on the Bund, in the British Concession, facing the Yangtze River. The Bund itself was something special. It had iron gates that were barred at night, and inside the gates the noise and dirt of the crowded Chinese city gave way to order and cleanliness and space. Green trees lined the wide streets and behind low walls stood the great English houses, encircled by verandas. Mrs. Tamplin's was the largest, and inside her private gate was a beautiful garden and the garden was part

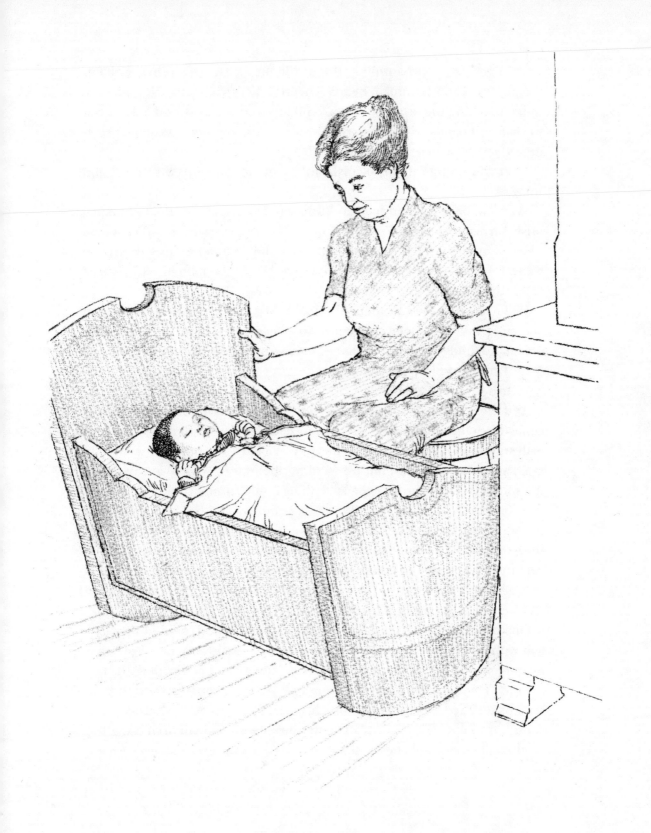

of the Christmas enchantment. But inside the house what other enchantment! Mrs. Tamplin, small, hearty, cheerful, her two brown eyes, one not quite matching the other but both twinkling and bright, stood at the door to shake all hands with her warm English grasp and her invariable greeting.

"Get your things off, my deahs! Santa's on the way—lots of goodies and things—"

We took off coats and hats and wandered slowly about the big luxuriously furnished rooms. Fruits and flowers were everywhere and coal fires glowed in the English grates under the tall mantelpieces. Slowly we walked, feasting our eyes until we came at last to the immense Christmas tree, surely bigger every year than the last.

When everybody was there the party began. Games and music and surprises followed one another at Mrs. Tamplin's imperious and kind command until the hour grew late. Then we heard the tinkling of bells and Mrs. Tamplin held up her finger.

"Hush—Santa's come!"

And there he was, miraculously behind the tree exactly as though he had come down the chimney, fat, red-cheeked, clothed in scarlet and sprinkled with snow and his pack as big as himself. We knew of course he was really good stout Mr. Tamplin but we wouldn't believe it. And what toys came out of the pack, beautiful expensive things our parents could not buy for us, wonderful dolls and paint boxes and engines and books, toys we had never heard of and certainly never dreamed of possessing! And after that, the wonderful cakes and candies and ices which Santa insisted must all be eaten up! Dear Mrs. Tamplin, wherever you are lying now, your soul is in heaven forever because once you made heaven come true for little alien children growing up in a foreign land.

Our own Big Party is a modest affair by comparison, held in the barn and without any luxury at all. But the same reckless joy attends. We begin inviting people the day after Thanksgiving and go on inviting until the last minute. The barn is a place for rough play but we dress it up with pine boughs touched with a silvered brush, and we go into our own woods and cut a big pine tree to stand beside the fireplace. The children hang the bright balls and tinsel and the lights and between the great beams we hang the mistletoe. We heap red apples in a wooden trough and pile the fire-place with logs, and wait for our guests at dusk. By some Christmas magic it almost always snows that night and our guests arrive red-cheeked and powdered with snowflakes.

The Big Party is a reckless affair. Everybody has invited everybody and we never know or even try to know how many people are coming. People begin to gather upon the hour and they stay late. Babies, who cannot last out the evening, for everybody brings the babies, can sleep on cushions on the floor. The fun begins when there is a crowd. It used always to be marionettes when our children were little, but now they feel too grown-up for the miniature plays. Sometimes we have a full-size play, put on by the high school children, sometimes we invite guests from abroad to entertain us, and perhaps there is a motion picture and certainly there is music. The formal entertainment must not last too long. When it is over we have the first installment of food—chicken sandwiches, homemade cake and cook-ies, nuts and punch and coffee, and then the dancers take the middle of the floor and everybody else sits in a circle around to watch.

The floor was made for roller skating on rainy winter days and for basketball and volley ball or just ordinary rough-housing. On this night of the Big Party, though, we have polished it up for dancing. The band plays more and more frantically as the night goes on, and young people tend to forget that parents sit in the circle. In the corners of the big barn, behind the backs of parents, small fry entertain themselves happily with wrestling and rough-housing, and the babies sleep peacefully on.

It has to end sometime. The band remembers that it is long past mid-night, mountains of sandwiches have sunk down and the punch bowls are low. Outside, the snow is piling deep. Sleepy babies are lifted from their pillows and small children sticky with lollipops are forced into warm coats and only the young men and women linger. Yet even they must part, for tomorrow is here and it is already Christmas Eve. The hubbub dies down and finally only the family is left. We put out the lights and cross the snowy lawn, and once more the Big Party takes its place in tradition and in memory.

Most of the year our house is a quiet place, though we have many children and grandchildren, and they have many playmates and school

71

fellows. We live in the country in the middle of land enough so that we hear no noise except from an occasional airplane, soaring near the sun. Woods divide us from the distant road and it is not a noisy road at that. The house is sprawling enough to provide everyone with his own room and the television, against which the elders are still rebellious, is relegated to a small tuckaway place in the last ell under the big walnut tree. The barn is the place for noisy games and the record player. There is no law against laughter and children's voices anywhere and these are loudest at croquet and tennis or in the small swimming pool. The baseball field is beyond the barn and the 4-H teams from neighboring villages make merry there without disturbing the peace of the house.

In winter the outdoor silence deepens. The barn may be full of noise on a Saturday but the windows are shut against the cold. In the house itself, except at evening, everybody pursues his own interest. The library chairs are draped with lanky legs and tousled heads. Somebody is making cookies in the kitchen. An artist works at his desk in his own room. Even the visiting babies busy themselves with the toy cabinet in the living room, maintained especially for them. We meet and share meals or games, but we are a busy family, with many interests, some shared, some solitary, all engrossing. I am sometimes surprised, myself, in the midst of my work at my desk, to listen and hear not a sound. I get up and go out in search of children and find them absorbed with pets or play or books or music or gardening. One tall boy is always to be found at the dairy barn, another is likely to be in the play barn with the records. A young daughter has a couple of the babies in tow. Even when there is no school, everybody is busy at something he wants to do.

As Christmas comes near, everything changes. We believe in Christmas, every one of us. We cherish every custom of world and family. Ever since our present teenagers had their first winter, we have done exactly the same things every Christmas, and yet each year we have always added something new. For us Christmas is far more than a day or two. It begins weeks ahead, privately even before that. But we have agreed not to let it emerge full-fledged until the day after Thanksgiving. To be fair, we decided years ago that we must give Thanksgiving Day its due as a day especially for America, our own country, and we devote ourselves to the day heartily

72

enough. Grownup children bring their little children, and together we sit down to a table stretched to its limit and beyond, so that we have to add the Pembroke at one end. The turkey raised upon our farm makes his appearance, inferior only infinitesimally to his brother, whom we are saving for Christmas, and mince pies take his place in the oven. A family football game follows dinner, for being country folk we dine at mid-day and sup at night.

Whenever I think of it, I realize again that Christmas in our house really began decades ago in that far-off other land of mine, in China. We seldom thought or spoke of being American and we did not feel solitary. I especially did not feel so, because then I had known no other country and had no other people. Only at Christmas did I feel, through my parents, the reality of my own land across the sea and another people, unseen and yet also mine. The rest of the year I came and went among the Chinese farm families who lived at the foot of the low hill upon which our house was built, played happily with little Chinese girls, and always spoke Chinese except to my parents.

At Christmas there was a difference even beyond the party at Mrs. Tamplin's house. My Chinese playmates knew nothing about Christmas except that it was a foreign festival. They were polite and accepted small gifts of love which we made to them, but still they did not know what Christmas was. True, the people in my father's church celebrated in their courteous fashion the birth of an unknown god-man some two thousand years ago. Rather awkwardly they added this day to the other good days in the year. The Christmas story was not entirely strange to them, for Chinese history is full of god-men, born of virgin mothers, who, performing their daily duties in home or field or by the clothes-washing pond, were visited in a solitary moment by a god. Their sons, thus conceived, were always men of genius and valor and righteousness with all the power that flows from that invincible combination.

True, we Americans thought our god-man was different and even better. My father taught us so. In spite of all, the god-men of the Chinese were, he said, heathen, and not the beloved and only begotten son, who bore upon himself the sins of the world. It was a long time before I understood that god-men always bear upon themselves the sins of the

73

world. It was Confucius who said, five hundred years before Jesus was born, "The inferior man blames others, but the superior man ever blames himself." Here in my American home, I have brought my children up on that profound truth until now when I begin to speak it they join in and chant it with me. I suppose they grow weary of it. I used to grow weary of the precepts of my own youth, yet I have remembered them.

It is strange how at Christmastime the old memories of life now gone come flooding back to me. It is more than a life gone—it is a world gone. The world we live in this Christmas is not like any other we have ever known. How many mothers and fathers weep, as we do in our hearts, when we watch our tall boys reaching up the Christmas tree to hang the tinsel and the silver balls! Another Christmas and where will they be? What is this world which we have made where the young can no longer count upon their future? God forgive us all, how have we let it come to this?

Yes, the children trim the Christmas tree now. We parents used to do it, waiting until night and the last excited child was in bed, and then shutting all doors, we wrought in secret, as all parents do on Christmas Eve, the eternal magic of Christmas morning. Long past midnight we worked, once until nearly dawn when four scooters brought and hidden away weeks before turned out to be not ready to ride, as we had supposed, but knocked down and to be assembled. We assembled them somehow and they stood scarlet bright beneath the tree before we slept. That last moment, when the tree is finished, and we stand to see what we have made, each year more beautiful to us, is a sacred one, consecrating anew love and home. We feel the house alive in every stone and beam and threshold.

The Christmas tree itself is an object sacred in every home. Even in China we always had a tree, a tree of some sort, sometimes a bamboo when pines were lacking. A bamboo makes a delicate fairy sort of Christmas tree. Its slender branches will not bear much weight. They do not break but they bend low under the smallest gifts. The leaves, too, curl very soon, and turn a silver gray. But the skeleton is beautiful, the branches symmetrical, and the jointed trunk is strong. One thing America has given to China, as Germany gave it to America, is the Christmas tree. There are many Chinese children who love the brightly lighted tree as well as Ameri-

74

can children do, and in many homes, even where the Birthday is not known, the tree is placed, surrounded with sweets and colored fruits.

Every year my parents raised the tree in our little church on a Chinese street and invited the people to come in. That was pleasant enough and there was a plenty of peanuts and candy and oranges for the children. But for me the heart of Christmas was not there. It was always in our own home, on Christmas morning, with no one but our small family gathered about our little tree. The gifts were few and it did not take long to see them all. But we lingered and then the talk began about America, the country I did not know, but to which I belonged. It was on Christmas morning that I knew my parents could be sick with longing for their own country and their own kind. I did not suspect it at other times, when they were busy and often gay. But on Christmas the glow of the tree shed its light across the sea, and in that glory I saw the beloved land and the people who were my own. It was a magic land and of course it did not really exist. There never exists such a land as the exile remembers on Christmas morning. It is dream country, and its citizens are angels. I am here now, in the land of my ancestors, and yet on Christmas mornings even yet, especially when the snow falls over our rolling countryside and we wake to a white Christmas, I am homesick for the magic land I used to think America was, a land where all is peace and men are truly brothers. Surely sometime? O Christmas, come, when our tall sons need not face the darkening future and life cut off! O Christ Child, show us that such things need not be! We are so skilled in war, so fumbling in the ways of making peace. We choose the easy way, and for this we shall not be forgiven. Of those to whom much is given, much is expected. At Christmastime I know again what I have always known. In the midst of joy, in the safety of our home, among our living children, I feel the anger of the world descend upon us, who have been given much, and yet have not found the ways of peace. The old wise words come back to me again, "The inferior man blames others, but the superior man ever blames himself."

I blame myself, my own, and the bitter taste of a Christmas long gone comes back again into my mouth, a year when I was only twelve.

We lived then in a part of China where the land was rich, and near a great and thriving city at the crossroads of the Yangtze River and the

75

Grand Canal. Because of our plenty there came from time to time into our region hordes of famine-stricken people from the north, where the Yellow River often overflowed its banks. That year the people came south a few weeks before Christmas. Thousands and tens of thousands swelled into hundreds of thousands. They built miserable huts, no larger than coffins, for winter shelter and they begged in swarms upon the streets and they poured through the city gates into the fertile valleys outside the walls and begged at farmhouse doors. Our house, like every other, was surrounded by a protecting wall, and front and back there were the stout gates, usually left unlocked in the daytime though always barred at night. Now we had to keep them barred by day as well, for though my parents worked night and day with the relief forces in the city, with the Buddhists and the Taoists and the Catholics and the other Protestants, and all such good people, to relieve the starvation that killed many hundreds every day, it was not enough. The people had waited too long. They had clung too desperately to their land and only when the children were dying did they set out on foot for the south. We forgot Christmas that year and all its plans and hopes. I saw my mother working all day at great cauldrons of rice, and at night she and my father put on ragged Chinese garments and went out among the huts to put a silver dollar into each doorway, hiding their faces so that none would know they were Americans, lest in their despair the hordes of starving break into our gates and destroy us by day. We scarcely slept and we ate the same food we prepared for the hungry.

Yet every morning the dead were lifted from our gates as they were lifted from every gate every day. They came to beg, to beat upon the locked gate with their last strength and then to die there. We dared not open to them, no one dared to open the gate of a house, for the starving would fall upon the house as locusts fall upon a field of wheat. I have tried sometimes to tell Americans how human beings behave when they are starved, but I cannot get them to understand. One has to see to know. And bitter above all is the needlessness of such suffering. China never starves entire. She has riches of food. But she has never in modern times had a government which carries food from one place to another for the people. When will we learn that there need be no starving anywhere in the world? In one country food is thrown away, in another the people die, today, as

76

then. May we be forgiven for not seeking out the ways of peace!

That Christmas when I was twelve the blessed day drew near in spite of the agony of the people. A week before Christmas, I remember, I asked my mother, "Shall we not have the tree this year?"

My mother was exhausted and she did not look up. She stood beside the big earthen stove in the outside kitchen where the cauldrons were steaming with hot rice gruel.

"What tree?" she asked. Her eyes were blank.

I could not answer. It was the final proof of the frightfulness of the days. My mother had forgotten Christmas.

I went away and wept. Never again was the world the same. I had been suffering and it had changed life for me. I understood from that day, I think, that suffering and starvation anywhere in the world affect everybody upon the earth. Sooner or later, and I pray not too late, we shall all know it.

I said no more about Christmas, I remember. Instead I plunged into helping my parents with all my twelve-year-old strength. Our utmost could not meet the dreadful need, but we did what we could. On Christmas Eve my mother remembered and said, "You see, children, that we cannot have Christmas this year. Instead of the nice things we usually eat, we must share the food of the poor, and instead of gifts to each other we will give what we have to buy more rice."

So there was no tree that year, no gifts, no Christmas feast. Christmas Day was spent like the other days before and after it, and yet it was a day different, too, from any of them. Among the starving who lay at our gates a little baby was born. As it was with that other child of Bethlehem whose mother "laid him in a manger, because there was no room for them in the inn," my mother took the young woman into our gate and the baby was born in our house. The baby was dead a few minutes after he was born. Neither did the young mother live. Where the father was we did not know. We did not know their names. We buried them in the Christian cemetery, nameless, and the dust of these two, the unknown mother and child, lay mingled with the dust of Christians. Somehow that gave comfort to my mother, for she had wept terribly when the baby died. He was just a little handful of bones. There was nothing with which to begin life.

"You simply cannot think of such things," people have said sometimes when I have tried to tell this story. But I have not learned how not to think of them. I cannot forget. Today in my own country, at this Christmastime of joy and wonder, I think of them. For the mother and child were not beggars. They were not thieves or wastrels. They were simply people who had nowhere to lay their heads. While others ate they starved, through no fault of their own. They could have been fed, and all like them can be fed. The earth has riches of food not yet tapped and the sea has untouched stores. We have never really tried to feed the hungry. Now, every Christmas at the hour when the tree is trimmed and the children are asleep, when our house stands waiting and at peace, I remember the mother and the child and I dedicate myself anew. They are not dead but living, alive in the haunted and hungry peoples of the earth, who die upon the doorsteps.

I have told our children about the mother and child. In a way the story has become part of the Christmas spirit in our house, so that Christmas here has become more than a festival of merriment. It has become, too, a time of sacrament, a remembrance of things yet to be done.

I suppose that it was the nameless mother and child who made us receive, one Christmastime, two little children who had no home, for whom in this vast and beautiful country of ours there was no room at the inn. From time to time, during the years I have lived in this farmhouse, which more than any other spot in the world has become for me my home, I have received letters from unknown persons asking me to find somehow a place for a little homeless child. There is always the same reason why no home has been found and they appeal to me as a last resort, "hoping," the letter always reads, "that you can perhaps find some Asian family who might be willing to adopt the child."

This means that the child has the blood of Asia in him. But it is not pure blood. It is half American. Before he was conceived somewhere a young man and a young woman met and mingled their blood, through love, which knows neither East nor West, and then there was born the child, and both East and West reject him. "We do not want to adopt a child with any white blood in him," a Negro woman once wrote me, whose husband is Chinese. "The white blood always predominates."

78

"We do not want any child with Asian blood," the white woman writes. "Oriental blood always predominates."

The predominating blood, I have learned, always means the blood that bears the weight of prejudice, the color that is despised. And so the little child, not wanted at the inn, is homeless among the millions of homes in the world, the millions of families who close the door.

I think what happened in our house began on that earlier Christmas of the mother and child who died in China. At any rate, one particular letter came to us one Christmas season telling of a child, whose father was Asian and whose mother was American, a little boy only fifteen months old, with brown skin and great black eyes and curling black hair.

We had thought our family was finished. Our children were growing up and our house was full, or so we thought. I know now that the house is never as full as one thinks.

I read the letter aloud to the children. It said quite clearly that unless we could find an adoptive home for the child, he would be put in a Negro orphanage. Now an orphanage is bad enough but a Negro orphanage is worst of all for a little boy who is not a Negro. For me all human creatures are valuable alike, and a black skin, a brown, a white, are the same in beauty. But there is a curse here in our land, a shameful prejudice against some, and our little boy, because of his lovely gold-brown skin, might be forced, if he were thought a Negro, to grow up under that burden of prejudice which no child should have to bear. He was, the letter said, a child of unusual heritage and intelligence, else they would not have bothered to write to me.

"What shall we do?" I asked the children.

They answered with silence and thoughtful eyes.

"What shall we do?" I asked the father of the family.

"It doesn't seem right to let him go to that orphanage," he said.

The house was already full of Christmas. We had cut the Christmas trees ourselves from little trees planted years ago, one big tree for the barn party and a slender and graceful one for the house, where the ceilings are low. Under the beds and in closets there were the piles of Christmas presents ready and wrapped. On the dining room mantel the holly made a background for the little straw angels and reindeer and Santa Claus in

79

his sleigh that we had once brought home from Sweden when the children were babies. The four-colored paper birds hung swinging below from the beams, and straw and tinsel stars shone there, all made by farm folk in Sweden for their own homes at Christmas.

We hurried home from Sweden that year earlier to get back in time for Christmas. We were not travelers when the children were small, believing that parents belong at home, but we were once compelled to make one hasty journey across the Atlantic. During the brief busy days in Stockholm we took time to buy gifts for everybody and especially we bought the little straw angels and Santa in his sleigh with his reindeer, and yes, some straw pigs to trot behind the angels on the mantel, and the straw and tinsel stars. They have become part of our American Christmas now.

Could we take another child?

We had cut the holly from our own holly trees and at the big front door the huge wreath with the red ribbon hung from the brass knocker. The wreaths are always hung at all the windows the day before the Big Party, so that the lights shine through them to welcome all our guests. The red candles were in the silver candlesticks and the turkey was stuffed and the plum pudding made and the Christmas music waiting to be sung and sung again. We begin singing Christmas Carols after Thanksgiving. Someone hums a tune, there is a catch of music from upstairs, and, listening, I hear "O Little Town of Bethlehem." The music swells as the days pass and long before Christmas we gather at the piano at night before we go to bed and sing the Christmas songs. Long ago in China I had learned to love Christmas carols sung under our windows by Chinese school boys, the children of those who had forsaken their own gods to follow the god-man of other lands and white-faced strangers. I first heard "O Little Town of Bethlehem" in Chinese, and from Chinese children the song rose out of the night, "Oh come to my heart, Lord Jesus, There is room in my heart for Thee." That made Christmas belong to everybody in the world.

"We must do whatever you think right," the father of the family said. Our smallest child, a blue-eyed, brown-haired daughter, crept into my room one night. "Mother, we will have to take that baby or I won't have a good time this Christmas," she said.

So with the approval of all I wrote the letter that brought him to us, a

80

tiny dark child in the middle of the night, given to us by kindly strangers who went away again and left him, a little silent bundle of woe, his eyes enormous, and he sucking desperately on a small thumb that seemed permanent in his mouth. I took off his coat and cap and held him close for a long time. He did not cry or speak. He was like a little animal, stricken to stone with fear. I have seen a baby rabbit stop like that in the field when the dogs came by.

I carried him upstairs and we undressed him and washed him and put him into the crib we had brought down from the attic, and laid him there. Still there was not a word and still the thumb was in the mouth and great dark eyes stared at one face and then another. One by one the family went to bed and I sat there alone with the baby. I let the light burn low so that there would not be darkness and so that he might see me, and I sang a little to him now and again. Once or twice he began to sob softly, and then he put out his other hand, the one he could spare, and I took it and held it and after a long time he slept. Some of the pain of that Chinese mother and child, now so long dust, was taken away from me that night.

The baby is a little boy now, his fears are gone, and he is happy and hearty. Life will not be easy for him and he will have to be strong enough to meet in other ways the burden that he escaped when he did not go to the Negro orphanage. But perhaps the world will be better by the time he grows up. It must be better, or we shall destroy each other with hate before that day.

Once the door opens, it is never closed again, of course. That is true of hearts as well as houses. The very same Christmas season a baby was born in a hospital not far from our house, and again he was one of those who belong to both sides of the world, his father Asian, his mother American. We did not hesitate this time. We sent for him at once and he was given to us because there was no place for him to go. We even had to send clothes for him, for he had none of his own, just the cotton shirt that hospital babies wear. It was fun to buy a layette again, and to have a tiny baby in the house who looked at me with Chinese eyes. I realized suddenly that, happy as I had been, I had missed my other people, too, and I was glad to have my Chinese-American baby. Today he runs everywhere, and talks incessantly, a child of gaiety and darting mischief, daring everything and fearing nothing.

Our new babies stayed in our house for three months while we planned how to keep them always. Had we been younger, my husband and I, we would have become their adoptive parents. But parents must be young enough to see babies through to the years when they are grown and can take care of themselves, and we were not young. Good grandparents we could be, and so we decided that we would find younger parents for them near us, where we could still be one family. A find old farmhouse stood empty in the middle of our farm and next to our own house. It had belonged to other people now gone and was for sale. If we could find parents and they would live there, it would be almost like keeping the babies in our own house.

We thought of all our young friends. The parents must be kind, and wide of heart so that these little children would not seem strange to them. They must belong to this region, deeply rooted here, so that the children could put down roots, too. Here where we live we are surrounded by Quakers and Mennonites of both the old and new variety. We thought of them and the thought began to center upon a certain two whom we had known for years enough to know them well. If they were willing, they were the ones.

We talked with them long one night and they held the babies while we talked. They did not decide at once for they are careful people, steadfast when they have made up their minds. But one day a few weeks later they came back. "We have long wanted to do something more as our share in the world's life," they said. "We think this is it."

And so it came to pass. Friends everywhere in the community helped to buy the house and furnish it simply. The parents brought their things, too, and one day in the spring we took the babies up the field path to their own home and their parents. We named it Welcome House. The babies can run across the field themselves now to Gran and Grandaddy's house, and they spend every Sunday here, and Christmas joy repeats itself every day and especially on Sundays, when they come to spend the day and the dining room table stretches its full length for all the growing children.

Staunch friends stand by to make Welcome House secure. What the house needs someone finds for it. The children live a natural family life, brothers and sisters from everywhere, but all Americans, for in America all were born.

The doors that Christmas opens never close. Five more times the door of Welcome House and of our hearts has opened for other children, a darling little Japanese-American girl, three more sturdy Chinese-Americans, and now within the last month, our tiny Korean boy. American though the children are, nurtured in the good ways of American life, we teach them, too, of their other lands, the great and ancient civilizations of Asia, the mother lands of the earth.

They give as they receive. They bring gifts to our community, to our homes and school, and the church where their parents take them on Sundays, and these gifts are the lively intelligence of India shining through our first child's dark eyes, the gaiety of China in the mischief and fun which make the nature of our second child, the dainty grace of Japan in our tiny girl, the health and heartiness of China, too, in the older three, and all the dignity of Korea, the Land of Morning Calm, is in our baby's noble head. It is our hope, our dream, brightened by every Christmas together, that our world-children, as we call them, will be the sort of people the world so sorely needs, the ones who understand both East and West, who belong to both, and who therefore can bring the two hemispheres together in peace. We believe that when children are brought up so to be, that they will so continue.

This is our Christmas faith. In a way it is already being fulfilled. I have spent the last hour holding our little Korean boy in my arms and thinking across the years. Here into this quiet American countryside, where a handful of years ago no one ever thought of Asia, the world is beginning to penetrate. The war really began it, I suppose. From here as elsewhere the farm boys, the village sons, went to China and the Philippines, to India and Japan and Korea, and some of them came back again. The son of my neighbor said, "I hate to think of our men fighting in Korea. The folks over there were mighty nice to me. Wonderful they were, really, so gentle and sort of cultivated, if you know what I mean."

"I do know," I said.

Yes, I know. I have watched the magic of our Korean baby. He looks

83

very Oriental, his skin is a dark cream, his large eyes are almond-shaped, and he has a great dignity. He looks like a young Buddha. My friend who has never seen such a baby seems a little afraid of him. She thinks he looks strange, perhaps, not like the babies she knows. But that lasts only a few minutes. He smiles, he reaches for her necklace, her brooch, he coos and answers her baby talk, and she says with surprise, "He's really like any other baby, isn't he?"

"Yes, he really is," I answer.

I know that the alchemy of human brotherhood is beginning to work in her. It always does if we do but meet face-to-face. We soon cease to see the shape of eye or the color of the skin. The love that Christmas stirs in the heart lives beyond the day and becomes a part of life. That is the purpose and meaning of Christmas and Christmas is fulfilled only when love lives on into life, the good love, the world love.

Christmas morning has become more for us, then, than just the day when we as a family among families rejoice. It has changed, of course, through the years. When our children were little, the day began strenuously. There were then four little ones and the middle-sized one, and the little ones woke at dawn. We learned through experience that the temper of the day lasted better if we had breakfast before we opened the big door to disclose the tree. The compromise was and still is that we have the stockings first, and then we all hurry through breakfast together. The stockings hang under the living room chimneypiece, a nice long line of them, very slack when they are hung on Christmas Eve after the carols are sung and just before the goodnights are said. They are very full on Christmas morning. The stockings are sacred to Santa Claus. The middle-sized child, who is now full-sized and only gets home for a day or so from her job, helps us to fill them. The teenagers are still children at Christmas and are sent early to bed. In the stockings are the small things, the tiny toys, the unusual sweet, the candy cane, the doll, the precious bit of jewelry that might be lost in the profusion of the tree. It was in the toe of my own stocking that I once found my gold thimble and another year my string of pearls. In the toe of her Christmas stocking the blue-eyed child found the ring she wanted, and there the boys found their first watches.

Christmas breakfast is a hasty affair of scrambled eggs and bacon and toast and coffee, with orange juice gulped down between and never mind washing the dishes. We have no helper in the kitchen or anywhere around the place on Christmas Day. We believe everybody ought to be at home that day and so we serve ourselves. It is an uneasy feeling to have lonely souls in the house longing for their own homes and families, while they are compelled to service. It clouds the pure joy of the house. Let each serve himself on Christmas Day.

The turkey is ready, stuffed the day before. I put him in the oven after breakfast and set the temperature for a long quiet baking for the solitary bird. Then we crowd through the living room together and the father slips in first to light the tree and to push back the sliding doors to the library, where the tree stands. It was not always a library. In the days of small children it was the playroom, but the years went by and toys became games and so we moved the playroom to the barn and lined the old room with bookshelves and made it the family library. Such now it is, and the tree stands between the two French windows that look into the court. For a moment no one moves. The sight is so old, as old as my childhood in China, and yet it holds for us all the magic it has for the youngest, for whom it is the First Christmas. The children trim the Christmas tree nowadays and the trimmings are as familiar as the house itself. We have the blue angel that we have always had and the colored balls, renewed only when one falls to the floor in silvery shatters, and we never try any new or modernistic trimmings. We want the tree to look exactly the same every Christmas, exactly as the oldest child remembers it looked the first time she saw it, and that is the way it is. Under the tree among the heaped gifts is the tiny crèche, the manger lighted by a star, and our children, from the oldest to the youngest, kneel before it to look in wonder and tenderness. It makes the old story come alive again more than words can do. Yet even so, it would be only a pictured scene did we not have the experience of our world-children. When another world-baby finds us somehow and is laid in my arms and our children gather around to see the newly born, we live the Christmas story in our own house.

"Aren't you afraid?" Someone is always asking that.

"Afraid of what?" I ask in reply.

The answer is always something different and yet it is always the same.

85

Afraid of taking in strangers, afraid of responsibility, afraid of your "own" children marrying or wanting to marry one of the "others" someday, afraid of the trouble, the worry, the care of them all. The answer is that I am afraid of nothing of the sort. I might be afraid if it weren't that I have found so many people who feel just as we do and who welcome the world-children with us. If you cannot believe it, then you do not know our community.

The spirit of good William Penn still lives among us, he who would not war against the dark-skinned Indians because he took them for his brothers. Here in our community there live those who still so believe that all men are brothers, and to the world-children they stand as kinfolk and friends, and to us as advisors. Quietly a small but strangely steady stream of money flows into the bank. Long ago those who followed the Star brought gifts of silver and gold to the Child, and he was the first world-child of all. They bring gifts today to our world-children, precious myrrh of friendship with its comfort for sorrow, for these children of the world must meet their own sorrows; and they need friends as well as family, and fragrant frankincense for joy, for the world-children, if they are loved enough, are joyful children. Around our tree gathers all the world family, father and mother and children, and we are the grandparents and our children are the near and younger kinfolk.

It is an all-day affair, this Christmas Day, and we stop for the dinner as usual in the middle of it. The turkey has done his duty in the oven, submitting with the best possible grace to being roasted tender and crisply brown, and the stuffing is made from our own Chinese chestnuts, gathered from our trees in the autumn. Christmas perhaps starts as far back as that, when the first frosts fall and chestnut burrs split open and the whole family takes baskets and puts on thick gloves and goes across the creek to the opposite hillside to gather the nuts. They are so sweet that all they need is to be partially boiled, their shells slit to let out steam, and then peeled and crumbled and mixed with half a cup of melted butter, a little salt dashed in, and their richness permeates the bird. We do not bother with soups or other filling foods before the turkey appears. It would be an insult to his highness. While the last basting is done, the children fly about and set the long table in the dining room. Again we have to add a table

86

at the end for we number twenty or so when we sit down.

As the turkey proves his tender worth, we venture hopes that his relatives do as well on other tables. For three days ago we packed and sent boxes for our grown-up children and their families, for an uncle's house and an aunt's Christmas dinner. Each box held another turkey from our farm. The best gifts come, we think, from farm and garden, and tucked in around the turkeys are our own scrapple, a pound or two of our own sausage, a jar of cranberry sauce, some honey in the comb from our hives under the pear trees in the orchard, and a jar of our special horseradish-and-beet relish. We like thus to share our Christmas dinner.

Whatever we are elsewhere in life, in Christmas dinners we are conservatives and fundamentalists. We eat the orthodox food with turkey, American food. On other days our shelf of cookbooks from every country may provide us Chinese meals or Indian dishes or foods from France and Spain, but we are all-American on Christmas Day. No, wait—the dessert is plum pudding, which I make myself after an English recipe as old as *A Christmas Carol.* With complete lack of originality, somebody always says every Christmas at the dinner table, "There never was such a goose—pudding!" The turkey legs whittled down as to meat always go to keep the youngest quiet, a family tradition, for our earliest home movies show our two tall sons, on their first Christmas and then in rompers, chewing on the huge drumsticks. Pudding must be tasted by everyone unless he is too young for teeth. Then he gets only a taste of hard sauce.

Glazed sweet potatoes and a salad flank the turkey, green peas, perhaps —we allow ourselves some latitude on vegetables—and coffee for all afterwards, with Sanka for the tinies, for all are equal on Christmas Day, and the feast is over. Many hands of many sizes clear the table and wash the dishes and we talk awhile and Grandfather smokes a pipe and Grandmother steals a moment to look into some new books, and then the children can wait no longer. We go back to the blessed tree.

It is always night before we are done, and the last moments are drawn out as long as possible. The spreading branches are searched again and again for some lingering tiny parcel. We cannot bear to let the day end, and when all is over a child or two will feel the tree too dear to stand forlorn and stripped. He puts some boxes back, piles up some brightly colored books, rescues the prettiest ribbons, and kneels down before the crèche to live over again the precious day. I watch the face, absorbed in wonder, lit by the candlelight, dreaming. I do not ask what thoughts are shaping in that child mind. I know, for I myself have dreamed.

On Christmas night there is a special joy, no longer of anticipation, but now realized and satisfied. We know what we have been given and each one sits down to enjoy afresh the pleasure of the gift received and given.

"How did you know that was what I wanted?" the child asks the parent and the parent asks the child, and each replies, "I remember you said so long ago—oh, weeks—and I wrote it down."

There are gifts so good that they were not imagined possible, and then it is sweet to have it said, "I thought it looked like you."

We have no costly gifts. There are too many of us for that. Shoes have to be bought for many feet. Clothes are worn out quickly by healthy children and they eat prodigiously every day. We live plainly and we give simple gifts, made at home if possible. But there is always one special gift for each upon the tree.

It is not too late even in the darkness to try new skis if there is snow, or skates upon the pond, and to go to the barn to hear new records and dance awhile, or play basketball, Ping-Pong or volleyball, or roller skate. Christmas night is the night for everything, the fulfillment, the night of peace. Our world-babies fall asleep, clutching dolls and teddy bears, and the little ones hold horns and mouth organs and toy trucks and engines, and our middle-sized daughters try on new frocks and our boys their knitted gloves and woolen socks. Candies and cakes are tasted and cookies fill the bowl and nobody can think of supper, they declare, until after the little ones are asleep, they appear in the kitchen, young appetites in search of cold turkey.

We are all in bed by midnight. Christmas is over, the children sigh. And yet we know it is never over. As soon as one is gone, another one is born in hope and faith for yet another year. I steal about the silent house in dressing gown and slippers, looking into each face upon the pillow. Across the field in Welcome House our world-babies sleep, each in his bed and crib. We are one family, gathered here from over all the globe, in love. There is always room at our inn.

88

The Christmas
Ghost

"Where shall we put the big star?" Jimpsey asked.

Jimpsey was six years old. His real name was James Collingswood Brown, but he was called Jimpsey because his mother had said one day, when she was trying to button his coat, "Oh, please stand still, Jimmy—you're such a jimpsey, jumpsey little boy!" And from that day on he was called Jimpsey.

The star was almost as tall as he was.

"Let's have a big star," his mother had said last week, "a big star to celebrate this first Christmas in our own home."

The house was one they had chosen together, a farmhouse set in meadows, and they moved there in the autumn when the trees were red and gold, and already it was home. They had lived in the city before they found the house, but Jimpsey's father said a boy should grow up in the country where there was plenty of room and that was why they were here instead of there. Now it was Christmas Eve, and Jimpsey's father had just finished the star. It was made of five crossed pieces of wood, and on each piece of wood he had fastened electric lights. They stood around it to admire it, Jimpsey, his father, his mother, and Mr. Higgins, the hired

man. Mr. Higgins was old and bent over, but he had been Jimpsey's best friend ever since they had moved into the house in the country.

"Yes, it's such a big star, where shall we put it?" Jimpsey's mother asked.

"Let's think," Jimpsey's father said.

"Put it at the top of the big sycamore tree there by the front door," Mr. Higgins said. "Then the lights will shine clear down to the bridge."

"A good idea," Jimpsey's father said. "That's what we'll do."

The house stood on a hill and at the bottom of the hill was a brook and across the brook was a bridge. Jimpsey could see the bridge very easily now, as he jumped around the tree. It had three arches and it was made of stone, a pretty bridge, his mother said, and it was another reason she had wanted to buy this particular house.

Meanwhile the star was going up. First Mr. Higgins tied a rope around the middle of the star, then he fetched a ladder and set it against the tree, then he climbed up into the tree and Jimpsey's father lifted the star and Mr. Higgins pulled, until the star was high among the branches, facing the bridge.

"Beautiful," Jimpsey's mother said.

Mr. Higgins tied the star fast to a branch and then he climbed down carefully because he was quite old, and Jimpsey's father went into the house to attach the electric cord. In a moment the star was shining, and they all clapped their hands, and Jimpsey's mother sang "O Little Star of Bethlehem."

"Except this is a big star," Jimpsey said when she had finished.

"Quite right," his father said, "and now I must go about some Christmas business of my own."

"So must I," Jimpsey's mother said.

That left just Jimpsey and Mr. Higgins, and as usual they began to talk. That is, Mr. Higgins began to talk and Jimpsey listened. Mr. Higgins loved to talk, and Jimpsey liked to hear him, and so everything was all right. Mr. Higgins began:

"You see the big barn, Jimpsey?"

"I see it," Jimpsey said.

It was easy to see, for there it stood, not far from the house, a huge red barn with a slanting roof. It was made of stone and wood, and inside the big doors were piles of hay and straw.

"You see the bridge?" Mr. Higgins asked.

"I see the bridge," Jimpsey said. He could not see it too well now, for the sun was beginning to set and a faint mist was rising from the brook. Still, he could see the three arches and the curve over the water.

"Did you know a ghost walks betwixt the barn and the bridge at midnight of every Christmas Eve?"

"A ghost?" Jimpsey repeated in a small voice.

"A ghost," Mr. Higgins said firmly. "It's the ghost of my old friend, Timothy Stillwagon, who died several years ago, come the day after Christmas."

"Why does his ghost stay in our barn?" Jimpsey asked. He was not sure that he liked the idea of a ghost, especially on Christmas Eve and in his barn.

"It wasn't your barn in those days," Mr. Higgins said. "It was the barn of Timothy Stillwagon himself. He was the farmer here and he lived in the house here and he kept his cows in the barn here, and every Christmas Eve the two of us would walk together from the barn down to the bridge, at midnight, mind you, after he'd trimmed the tree for his children. I'd trim my tree for my children, too, my wife and me, and then I'd walk up to the hill to see his tree, and he'd walk back with me to see my tree, because my house is there by the bridge."

It was true that Mr. Higgins' house was there by the bridge. It was a small house, set in a small neat garden.

"Why did you walk to see your trees?" Jimpsey asked.

"Because," Mr. Higgins said, "whichever of the two of us had the finer tree, the other was supposed to buy him a cup of hot coffee at the village diner."

"Did you have the best tree, Mr. Higgins?" Jimpsey asked.

Mr. Higgins laughed in big chuckles. "Neither one nor the other of us ever got the cup of coffee, on account of we always thought each had the prettier tree. The end of that was that we'd walk back and forth betwixt the barn and the bridge arguing about it, until we could walk no more on account of the cold. And you'll be getting cold too, Jimpsey, just standing here listening to me talk about it. So go into the house before your mother calls you in."

"Good night, Mr. Higgins," Jimpsey said, "and I wish you a Merry Christmas."

"The same to you, Jimpsey," Mr. Higgins said. "And it will be a merry Christmas for me, because you are here. My

own children are grown up and gone away, my old wife is dead, and I'm alone yonder in that little house of mine by the bridge, as I've been for many a year. But this Christmas, bless you, when I look up here, I won't see a dark house. I'll see a warm house with a family in it, and you the child, and above the house a big star shining. Oh, Timothy Stillwagon and I will have something to talk about at last!"

Jimpsey was surprised. "You mean you still talk to him?"

"Oh, sure," Mr. Higgins said cheerfully, "him and me, we walk the road together, just as we always did on Christmas Eve, me in my flesh and bones, and he in his ghost."

Jimpsey heard this and he was not at all sure he liked the idea of a ghost walking this very night of Christmas Eve. He went into the house and shut the door tightly and ran to find his mother. She was in the living room tying silver balls on the Christmas tree.

"Mother!" he said in a little voice. "I'm here."

She turned around, surprised. "Why, Jimpsey," she said, "you look white. Are you cold?"

"No," Jimpsey said. "It's just that Mr. Higgins says we have a ghost."

"Do we?" she said. "Well now, who is he?"

"He's a man who used to live here, Mr. Higgins says, but now he's a ghost."

His mother laughed. "Oh, that Mr. Higgins—he does talk so much!"

"Don't you believe him, Mother?"

"Not when he talks about ghosts," she said and she tied another silver ball on the tree.

At this moment from upstairs Jimpsey heard his father

96

singing a Christmas carol. It was his favorite, a cheerful one, the one about decking halls with boughs of holly, and Jimpsey ran upstairs.

"Daddy," he said all out of breath. "Did you know we have a ghost?"

His father was tying a red ribbon around a very small box wrapped in silver paper.

"Tell me about it," he said.

Jimpsey began all over again. "It's the ghost of Mr. Timothy Stillwagon. He lived in this house, him and his children."

"He and his children," his father said. "And I'm sure they had a happy life, and bless his ghost, and don't tell your mother you saw me wrapping this very small package because it's for her, and inside it is a beautiful gold bracelet made just for her."

"I won't tell," Jimpsey said and he stood watching his father tie a big bow on the small box.

"Are you afraid of ghosts, Daddy?" he said after a while.

"Well," his father said, "I've never seen one. It's silly to be afraid of something you've never seen. Fact is, Jimpsey, I don't even believe in ghosts."

"Mr. Higgins does," Jimpsey said.

"He's a lonely old man and maybe he dreams of ghosts to keep him company. And speaking of company, let's go downstairs and see if your mother needs help with the tree."

They went downstairs together and what with one thing and another, eating supper by the fire and having his bath and hanging up his stocking by the chimneypiece, Jimpsey went to sleep thinking about Santa Claus instead of Timothy Stillwagon.

"Go to sleep right away," his mother said when she tucked him into bed.

"Santa Claus has a lot to do for you tonight," his father said, kissing him good night.

How long he slept Jimpsey did not know. When he woke up the house was very quiet, so quiet that he thought he would get up and see why it was quiet. He put on his slippers and his warm red bathrobe and went to the window. The big star was still shining, so that Santa Claus could find his way, and shining so brightly that Jimpsey could almost see the bridge.

Then suddenly he saw the ghost. Slowly, slowly he saw a small figure walk out of the barn and down the road toward the bridge. He stared as hard as he could. Was it really—yes, it was really a ghost, a shadowy gray ghost in the light of the star.

For a minute Jimpsey wanted to run back to bed and pull the covers over his head. Then he remembered what his father had said. "It's silly to be afraid of something you've never seen." And instead of hiding himself in bed, Jimpsey decided then and there that he would go and look at the ghost and see whether he was to be afraid of it. It took several minutes to get into his clothes and his warm coat and his galoshes, for there was snow on the ground, but he managed. He slipped out the front door and he was glad the big star was shining across the meadow and on the road, so that he did not need a lantern from the barn. He

ran as fast as he could down the road, looking for the ghost. He could not see it. He couldn't see anybody or anything, just the snowy white road lit by the star.

Now he was almost disappointed. To be so near a ghost and then lose it! He stopped running and wondered whether he should just go home and back to bed. He was not afraid—oh, no—but everything was so quiet, and beyond the edge of the light from the star was the darkness. But Jimpsey was quite a brave boy at heart and he did not give up easily and soon he began to walk again toward the bridge.

It was a good thing that he did, for now he saw the ghost again. It was sitting on the wall of the bridge and it looked very small and tired and lonely. He was suddenly not afraid any more. He began to walk briskly until he reached the bridge. Then he stopped and looked at the ghost. The light from the star was dim now, for the bridge was rather far from the house, and he could not see the ghost very well. He stepped nearer and nearer until he was quite close. Yes, there the ghost was, sitting on the stone wall of the bridge.

Now at this very minute what should happen except a big sneeze! Jimpsey had forgotten to put on his cap and the cold wind was blowing around his ears and in his hair. At the sound of the sneeze the ghost gave a start.

"Why, Jimpsey," it said, "what're you doing here at this time of night?"

The voice was not the voice of a ghost—not at all. It was the voice of Mr. Higgins. The wind blew off the ghost's hat and under it was the face of Mr. Higgins, looking very cold and wrinkled.

100

"I wanted to see a ghost," Jimpsey said, "and it's only you, Mr. Higgins. . . . Isn't there any ghost? You shouldn't have said there was a ghost when it's only you, Mr. Higgins."

"Well, now, Jimpsey," Mr. Higgins said. "I'm ashamed I said there was a real ghost, when it's only Timothy Stillwagon's memory that I walk with on Christmas Eve. I guess I wanted to believe he walks with me every Christmas. Of course he can't walk in flesh and blood, the way he used to, and so I just made him into a ghost, because even his ghost would be more than nothing at all, you know. Yes, I guess it's only a memory I walk with, after all."

"What's a memory, Mr. Higgins?" Jimpsey asked.

Mr. Higgins picked up his cap and pushed it down over his ears. "It's something or somebody—you can never forget."

"Like the gray poodle dog we had," Jimpsey said. "He got sick and died when we were living in the city, but I don't forget him. His name was Buster. Is he a memory, Mr. Higgins?"

"Sure he is," Mr. Higgins said. "The same as Timothy Stillwagon. We were friends all our lives, him and me. We went fishing together when we were little boys, like you. We fished under this very bridge and caught catfish and took 'em home for supper. And we grew up and got married and had other little boys like you, and then one day it was all over and only me left—me and a memory. Timothy's not dead for me, Jimpsey. Come Christmas Eve, I walk the road from the barn to the bridge, and he walks with me as if he was alive again. Call him a ghost or not—

I see him this minute, as he was alive, because we were friends. As long as you remember somebody, he's still alive —in you, if nowhere else—eh, Tim, old boy?"

Mr. Higgins turned his head and smiled, exactly as if Timothy Stillwagon were sitting there on the wall beside him.

"Do you see him?" Jimpsey asked.

"I see him," Mr. Higgins said, "but that's because I know how he looked. You can't see him, because you don't know how he looked."

"You're not afraid?" Jimpsey asked.

"Of course not," Mr. Higgins said. "Do you think I could be afraid of Timothy? I never was nor am I now. As long as I live, we're the same friends we always were."

"But when you die, Mr. Higgins?" Jimpsey asked.

"Then you'll remember me, come Christmas Eve," Mr. Higgins said, "seeing as we're getting to be such good friends already. Christmas Eve is a great time for remembering friends—not just presents, you know, but thoughts —loving thoughts."

"I'll always remember you, Mr. Higgins," Jimpsey said.

"Good," Mr. Higgins said. "I'd rather have that for Christmas than a barrel full of presents." He got up. "That wall is sitting kind of cold under me. And you ought to be in bed. I'll take you back to the house. . . .You understand what I've been talking about, Jimpsey?"

"Kind of," Jimpsey said.

"It'll come clear to you some day," Mr. Higgins said.

He took Jimpsey's hand and they walked up the hill again, in the steady light of the big star, and when they came to the house Mr. Higgins said good night and Merry Christmas again and Jimpsey said the same to him. Then Jimpsey went upstairs and put on his pajamas. Just before he jumped into bed he looked out the window and saw Mr. Higgins, very small and bent, walking down the road to the bridge.

"So now," Jimpsey told himself, "some Christmas Eve when I'm as big as Daddy, maybe I'll look out this window and see the ghost of Mr. Higgins walking down that road. Only it won't be a ghost. It'll be my memory of Mr. Higgins."

He climbed into bed and pulled up the covers. Tomorrow he would have to explain to his father and mother—explain the Christmas ghost. Tomorrow—tomorrow—and suddenly he was fast asleep.

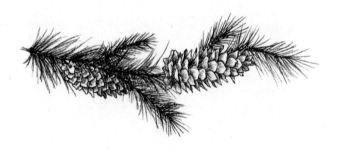

Thoughts of
a Woman
at Christmas

The blessed season of Christmas is rich with more than giving and receiving and feasting. Within these brief weeks, these certain days, are crowded the thoughts and feelings of many hundreds and even thousands of years of human living, a concentration of the deepest relationship of man and woman combined into family. Today, as I think of holly wreaths and gifts, I ponder again, as I have so often before, the scene of Mary and Joseph and the Child. There is pathos in that scene—or so I imagine. Generations of painters have portrayed the Holy Family, and their emotions and hidden feelings about Man, Woman and Child, the Holy Three, have flowed from the brushes they put upon canvas. The woman is the center and she it is who holds the Child. She has always the same face—calm, fulfilled, at peace. She has achieved the purpose for which she was created. She has created the perfect Child, a Son. Why a son and not a daughter? And why is the man Joseph always in the shadows? He is a patient, weary man, leaning upon a staff. He has a sober, dutiful air. He seems dubious of his part in the creation. And what indeed is the significance of the Woman, impregnated by divine spirit, so that her Child is not the son of the man who stands in the shadows? And why is this story universal to all religions, so that one finds it again and again in the ancient myths of every country? These are Christmas thoughts, penetrating deep into mysteries human and divine, and leading the thinker onward from that Holy Birth, so long ago, to the same three today, man, woman and child.

Pondering once more the face of the man Joseph, it seems to me, even at this distance, that while he loves the Woman and the Child, he is not quite sure of his place with them. She looks so confident of herself, so

sweetly proud of what she has produced. He wonders forever, perhaps, what he has to do with these other two, to whom nevertheless he is inescapably attached and for whose welfare he feels it his duty to work. I have seen many such patient Josephs, standing in the shadows behind the woman and the child. There is a patient Joseph hidden perhaps in every man, and I wonder if it is against this hidden Joseph in himself that every man at some time in his life rebels? I daresay that the first Joseph rebelled, too, in his quiet way. At least he seems to have stayed by his carpenter's bench while Mary went alone to follow her amazing Son. When she stood at the foot of the cross upon which the Son hung, another woman stood beside her—not Joseph. So I suppose Joseph went on with his own dogged life, dutiful and good.

Perhaps he was afraid of the Woman? Perhaps he still is. I have often been startled by a glint of fear in a man's eyes when he looks at a woman. He hastens to conceal it, but it escapes him. It is as involuntary as a dagger, half drawn and then thrust back. I am always sad to see that fear. Love should cast out all fear. Why then are men afraid of women?

The obvious answers are ready. Women are the disciplinarians in the house. They are the constant naggers, if not the final authority. Fathers seldom discipline their children in day-to-day ways. They profess weariness, they shrink from the task. Perhaps they, too, in their deep subconscious selves feel that the children belong to the women and not to them. It is easy to beget a child. It can be done without a thought and with little or no emotion. But to conceive a child is another matter entirely, and to live in closest communion and alone with an unborn child for nine months is an intimacy profound and formidable. No wonder that man fears woman and distrusts the child!

Nevertheless, in the practical everyday of home, somebody must teach and discipline the children, and when men dislike the task women do it perforce. Women always do what men dislike doing. Women are usually the teachers in school and it is sad for them that this is so, for what boy can love the creature who compels him to sit before a desk when his whole being longs for freedom? Man carries the sources of childhood rebellion in him as long as he lives, and rebellion against mother and teacher develops into rebellion, secret or overt, against wife. And she, alas, too often continues beyond the wedding day her role as disciplinarian and teacher, and is forlorn when she divines that love is gutted by fear. Forlorn because of course woman cannot respect man when she knows he fears her, and yet she longs above all else in life to respect man, knowing very well that without respect, love dies.

Are men afraid of women? The signs are here. It is to be seen in the gang spirit into which so many men retreat so that they think of enjoyment and relaxation only when they are with "the fellows," and away from the women in their homes.

Fear is in the ardor, too, with which many men continue to proclaim women's inferior achievements, and this in disregard of facts. How many men instinctively mutter their impatience with a woman driver, in face of figures which prove that women drive with fewer accidents, per capita, than men! And no less a man than Albert Einstein wrote in his book *Cosmic Religion* these pitiful, fear-revealing words:

"In Madame Çurie I can see no more than a brilliant exception. Even if there were more women scientists of like caliber they would serve no argument against the fundamental weakness of the feminine organization."

Remembering Madame Curie's unique achievments as a creative scientist while she performed also the tasks of wife, mother and housekeeper, I inquired recently of a friend who knew Einstein well whether his mind ever changed on the subject of woman. I was told that indeed there had been an occasion when, after reading Ashley Montagu's book *The Natural Superiority of Women*, the great man seemed about to announce a change in his estimate of half of the human race. Unfortunately, the friend said, someone entered the room at that moment and the important words were never spoken.

The real proof of man's continuing fear of woman, however, is most obvious in his tacit resolution not to allow her presence in the centers of policy-making. True, a woman is sometimes flaunted as token of man's tolerance. A woman or two on a governing board, otherwise male, serves the same purpose as a Negro or two. They are show pieces, signifying nothing, for generally speaking, the governing bodies of all organizations are still made up of men. It is true that men who are secure in their own positions, who belong to no minority group, who are successful as individuals in addition to being white, gentile, Protestant and male, do sometimes express fearlessly their high estimate of women. Even Bismarck, the Iron Chancellor, once said: "I respect every woman who elevates us men, teaches us religion and morality, preserves our ideals . . . I have long wished for the cooperation of women in politics. Mark my words, the day will come when women will be called to cooperate in politics. We men are all clumsy. We Germans especially are bears." And Ibsen once declared plainly that "women must solve the problems of humanity." Ibsen, says Professor Litzman, in his book on Ibsen, "put great faith in woman's power, unspent as it is, and drawn from fresh sources, for social work in companionship with man."

These are great men speaking and the average man has not their fearlessness and self-confidence. His fear is further proved by his continuing rejection even of the primary concept of human equality expressed in the Equal Rights Amendment [now passed] which year after year is denied approval by Congress, although surely there was never a more simple declaration that citizens should not be denied their human rights merely because they are women. True, there are also women who are opposed to the Amendment. Some women have the habit of inequality. They have no opinions of their own and, slavelike, merely echo the words of the men they know. Other women profit by special protective laws, not knowing that all persons, men and women, have the right to protective laws. Still others actually do profit by the segregation of women, even as some Negroes profit from racial segregation. In our interesting and complex national life certain persons benefit from inequalities and the limited competition that results from inequality anywhere.

Man's fear of woman is traditionally expressed, however, in the hackneyed statement that woman has not, and therefore cannot, create great works of art. She is not the creator, we are told. Well, she is of course the creator in the most basic sense. It is her nature to create. She receives into herself a bit of chemical material and from it she creates a human being. It may be asked, is this bit of chemical material an essential? Science whispers already that it is not. Years ago a scientist fertilized a rabbit's ovum with a simple assortment of chemicals from test tubes. He then

110

transplanted the ovum into a female rabbit's uterus and the baby rabbit developed normally and was born without benefit of father. It can be done, but let us pray that with the rabbit science halts. For his own happiness, man must remain essential, and therefore for woman's happiness. Happiness must be mutual or it becomes unhappiness.

And if it is a fact that woman has in later centuries created less vociferously in the arts than man, is it not because of the circumstances under which she lives? The first necessity for artistic creation is, surely, the free mind, the unhampered hands. Woman is not free either in mind or hand. She is busy with household cares and troubled by doubts about her duty. She sighs, "Oh, if only I knew what I was supposed to be, I could be it!" What she must know is that it is for her to decide what she wants to be. That she does not know what she should be is the result of a slave mentality which has invaded her mind in the centuries of man's domination. We will not know what woman can achieve until she frees herself from her own self-doubt. So long has she been told that she is inferior to man that she has come herself to think that she may be his inferior, and so, like a slave, to accept humbly the narrow space allotted to her. Mozart's sister was known to be more talented than he was, but their father would not allow her to continue her musical education, lest it take her beyond her "sphere." She submitted, trained in such deference, just as Chinese women in the not distant past themselves bound their daughters' feet even as their own feet had been bound, in spite of the pain and the crippling, and thought they were doing their duty.

The result of such inherited hopelessness in women is matched only by an equally reasonless and childlike conceit in men—reasonless, for the laws of inheritance apply equally to male and female, and childlike because it is ignorant and unthinking. A daughter has a chance, equal to the son's, of inheriting brains and even genius from their mutual ancestors. If she does not fulfill her inheritance it is not because it is not in her, but because her environment does not allow its development. In the slave labor that built the Great Wall of China, that dug the Suez Canal, that works in the camps of Communism today, there were and are men with high talent and some with genius who nevertheless have remained and will remain lost to the human race because they cannot fulfill their potentialities under the

111

circumstances in which they are compelled to live. In the same way among women there are many talented and even some of genius, in numbers proportionate to males, who, like slaves, are lost in the drudgery of kitchen and childbearing. Man's fear of woman has never found an expression more clear than in the old German clamor, renewed by the Nazis, of *"Kinder, Küchen und Kirche"* for women. I hear its reverberations sometimes in our own country. Indeed, even certain male psychiatrists who ought to know better are saying that women are discontented because their "sphere" is not defined. Better, these men say, that we return to the "certainties" of the nineteenth century. Yet anyone who has read and studied the books of the nineteenth century without bias must realize that while men may have been happy in an adolescent sort of way when women had a limited "sphere," the nineteenth century was bitterly unhappy for women and cannot therefore have been really happy for mature men. Indeed, the discontents that were expressed through feminism had their root source in the injustices of woman's life in the nineteenth century.

Yet the basis for woman's discontent, then as now, was not in revolt against man so much as in her loss of respect for him when she discovered his fear of her. For no one can respect the timid, and for woman, at least, love is based upon respect. She could not, she cannot, respect man when she knows he is so afraid of her that he thinks she is to be subdued by brawn and club. Crude force may make woman temporarily subject, but it never wins her respect or her love. The notion of a cave man dragging a smiling female by the hair to his cave is pure male fantasy—a wistful dream that never was or will be reality.

No, opportunities for women must not be curtailed in any field. They should be as limitless as the individual's capacity allows. We must not dream of the past, for such dreams are futile. "Old men dream dreams," the wise man of the Scriptures says, "but young men see visions." The past is of use to man and woman only when it provides a deepened understanding of the present. We must consult the past, if we are to know ourselves and what we are and why, but we can never and should never return to the past for our shaping of the present or for our visions of the future.

The changing relationships between men and women today the world over are but one aspect of the generally transitional age in which we live. We have not adjusted to each other, man and woman, any better than nations have adjusted to one another at this moment. We are prone to think of today as the norm and the permanent, but today is never permanent. It is only the link between yesterday and tomorrow and we must understand yesterday in order that we may live today without anxiety and face tomorrow without dread.

In spite of man's inarticulate and submerged fear of woman and his reluctance to consider her as fully human as he is, and in spite of woman's inadequately concealed contempt for men, I feel hopeful at the Christmas season, in this year of Our Lord. For in both man and woman today I discern a new and genuine desire for understanding each of the other that will produce in time a happier life for both. The situation is both sad and hopeful, sad because too often men and women in our western civilization do not enjoy their life together as they should, and hopeful because intelligent men and women really want to respect and enjoy each other. Modern man and woman earnestly desire a mutual happiness and actually neither wishes to dominate the other or limit personal liberty and growth.

I sat not long ago with a group of young men in New York and listened to their concern about women. Since they were all married, except one, and all had young children, they talked in terms of personal experience and I was impressed by their genuine love for their wives and their anxiety that their wives be happy not only in family life, but as human individuals. Their only question was, what did their wives want and how could what they wanted be provided within the framework of modern marriage and home and the necessity for man, at least while the children were young, to be the chief provider of funds? Personal happiness included the consideration, too, of sexual compatibility. The young husbands were frankly concerned about their own responsibility in this aspect of marriage. Until rather recently it has been taken for granted that the sexual satisfaction of the male in marriage has been the only necessity, since, it was thought, woman's satisfaction was chiefly in motherhood. The young husbands were patently somewhat frightened at the modern idea that woman also has personal sexual needs and that it is man's responsibility to see that she is satisfied. One young man in a sudden burst of distraction cried out:

113

"What with all this sex education in schools and books, the average man is afraid to get married! Why, the very idea that he is responsible for the woman's fulfillment is enough to make him impotent!"

The laughter which followed this outburst was laced, I felt, with ruefulness. No wonder our male psychiatrist speaks longingly of the nineteenth century, when women kept their sex needs, if any, to themselves. Sex in woman is a subtlety. A woman's femaleness is inherent in her whole nature, it permeates her dreams and her mental processes but, for her, sexual union is consummation rather than approach, demanding respect before love. I do not wonder that the average man fears woman. Time, effort and even some intelligence are required in order to comprehend her completely, and in our age, deeply influenced as it is by wars and military life, too many men have learned to enjoy only the simple and the crude. Indeed, it is doubtful whether women or men realize fully how much militarism affects their personal lives. To take but one example, when males are segregated into armies at a young age, before they have had time to become fixed in heterosexual patterns, it is inevitable and historically proved that there is great increase in homosexuality. Though this trait may not express itself overtly, and indeed usually does not, yet the homosexual image predominates in love relationships for many men long after their enforced segregation is over. Moreover, man's fear of woman is enhanced by his segregation from her, and fear of women, we are told by psychologists, is a significant reason, too, for homosexuality in men. And even though we may not be in actual war, the military draft does the same damage, for it demands the same separation from normal female companionship at a critical pattern-forming age.

The abnormal pattern expresses itself in curious ways. In a military age, for example again, men like women to look boyish. We see women slim themselves down into boylike figures, they cut their hair short, they become mannish, they tend to use the vocabulary of boys, they swear easily, they use four-letter words, they shed femininity. It is an unconscious process but none the less actual. In times of prolonged peace, especially when males are no longer drafted and the fear of wars has passed, the sexes tend again to assume their proper aspects, the men become masculine, the women feminine.

Nor is it men's latent homosexuality alone that tends to produce boyish women. While men are away at camp or at war, men's responsibilities are thrust upon women. Woman has to be father as well as mother. She learns to do man's work not because she likes to but because she must. She tries to do it as well as she can and takes a natural pride in her performance. When the man comes home again, she has to learn how to let him perform his share of the work. A pretty young wife discussing this with me the other day flung out her angry defense:

"He says I am not feminine, that I act like a man, that I'm too aggressive. *I* say that he unwomans me, because he doesn't do the man's work in the home, and I have to—somebody has to! We're always hearing about women unmanning men—well, men unwomen us! They don't do what they should do as men and then when we do as well as we can, they say we aren't womanly!"

The effect of militarism, or even of the threat of war which necessitates the continued segregation of young men before they are stabilized as males, is significant in still another effect. Men segregated into camps are with women in such short periods that they have no time for the prolonged relationship which results in the highest mutual satisfaction. Glands demand immediate relief, and men tend more and more to think of sex as one brief act rather than as a complex and fascinating communication, permeating every aspect of continuing interrelated life between man and woman. Since man is made self-centered and urgent because of his immediate physical need, he likes to think that woman is urgent, too. This has given rise to the curious fallacy, prevailing today even among specialists who should know better, that women are sexually as urgent as men. This is not true. It's a male wish.

Men and women are not the same, yesterday, today or ever. One is not inferior or superior to the other, and the brain capacity of each varies not with sex but with the individual. Yet man and woman are different not in what they think but how they think, not in essential action or need but in how action is performed, how need is met. The difference lies in how and not in what.

Moreover, man instinctively thinks of himself, but woman by nature is compelled to think beyond herself and for the child who may be born. An

115

instinct so profound is natural law. Everything in due course is woman's way, and her primary battle with man is on that score. She demands provisions and man avoids them.

Yet in her own fashion, merely by being all feminine, woman shapes man as much as he shapes her. Each has a common hope, and it is to please the other, and so to arrive at perfect companionship. Alas, because woman longs to admire and to respect in order that she may love, man has too often put on only the show of strength and wisdom. And woman, thus deceived, turns bitter and the bitterest creature under heaven is the woman who discovers that bravery is only bravado, that strength is only a uniform, that power is only a gun in the hands of a fool. She turns cold with bitterness and she resigns from life, and when she resigns from life, she merely goes through the motions of day and night. When a man complains that his wife has ceased to take an interest in life, that the marriage has become dull, then I know that his wife is not only resigned in spirit, but she has actually resigned from their marriage. Ah yes, there was a death struggle before she gave up. She was probably nagging and domineering and not very pleasant to live with—people who face death usually put up a struggle of some sort that is not pleasant to see. And when a woman gives up in marriage and becomes merely a house automaton, she usually gives up in the community, too. Society loses her and all her gifts. That is why women's votes have not changed conditions in our society. Woman goes to the polls in a lackadaisical mood. She chooses for superficial reasons. She knows she cannot accomplish anything real. She is not speaking for herself, she is merely choosing a man to speak for her. She has resigned from the actual.

It is of course not always the woman who gives up. Some women die less easily than others. They persist in struggling against death, and in the struggle it may be the man who yields first. He may become the automaton, and the more helpless he is, the more obedient to her self-protecting anger against him for his yielding, the more agonized she is. Here is woman's secret. When woman loses respect for man, it is not because she does not want to love him. It is because she cannot love him with her whole heart and her whole mind as she wants to love, for it is only when woman loves man thus wholly can she love him also with her body. And

116

it is basic for happiness in the human family that woman be able to love man physically, too. Contrary to superficial expert opinion, women do not want to mother their husbands. The concept of "momism" is male nonsense. It is the refuge of a male seeking excuses for his own lack of virility. I have listened to many women in various countries, and I have never found a woman who wants to mother her husband. The very idea is repulsive to her. She wants to mother her children while they are young, but never a man. She is often forced into the role of mother by man's weaknesses and childishness, and she accepts the role with dignity and patience, or with anger and impatience, but always with a secret profound sadness that is unexpressed and inexpressible. I hear my own housekeeper say sometimes, and too many times, "Oh, well, you know how men are. They never grow up." The words may be uttered with apologetic laughter and seeming good humor, but they do not conceal the hidden sadness. Woman wants to love man with respect and admiration. She wants to love him with utter confidence in his mature integrity.

I do not speak for woman alone. For man, too, is deprived of ultimate happiness when woman does not love him wholly. One-sided love is impossible. It cannot continue. Ultimately love dies without full response. Love must feed upon love. When, therefore, woman resigns and is resigned, she gradually ceases to love and therefore to respond and so by that very resignation, she dooms herself to lose man's love. When she no longer believes in him, he begins to be afraid of her and in turn he ceases to love her.

Sad it is that so many men are afraid of women and especially of the superior woman, the woman who has the most to give him. And strange to contemplate is the fact that, regardless of how oppressive man may be toward woman, women are never afraid of men. Explain me this truth for I do not know why it is true, except that in colonial countries where I have seen white men subdue black men and have seen the black men for the moment obedient, yet I have never seen the black men afraid. It is the white men who are afraid. Nor do women gang together as men do. They do not feel the necessity, for they do not need refuge. Women do not even defend women as men defend each other and, contrary to unthinking opinion, this is not because of jealousy. Women are not jealous of each

117

other. They like or dislike women as individuals, not because they are women. Women do not gang together even against men, for they are not afraid of men. And modern young women, I find, generally speaking, like to work for a good boss whether this be woman or man.

I reject the word *dilemma* for the situation in which men and women find themselves today. We are, I repeat, merely in a transition period, the transition from the matriarchal period of the dawn age of human life through the present patriarchal age to the age, yet to come, of complete cooperation between man and woman for their mutual benefit. It is a long development, and we must view it in perspective midway between past and future.

In the beginning, biologically speaking, there were not two sexes but one. For untold time life went on without the male. New life was created by the fusion and development of cells, by spore formation and virgin reproduction. When the male first appeared he was only a part of the female, a minute sac filled with·male seed. This stage can still be seen in primitive life, as for example in the barnacle, where the male is a parasite that lives only in the valves of the female. All male bees are drones and the only mosquitoes that live, however undesirably, are female, for the male dies as soon as the sexual act is over. Below the vertebrates, the female continues larger and stronger than the male.

Even human man, however, did not achieve his supremacy so long as he did not suspect that he was father to the child. For there was a long period when neither man nor woman knew that man was necessary to the creation of the child. Indeed there are some remote tribes upon the earth who today still do not know, or at least understand, the act of man's part in life. It was woman who, in the beginning, first began to wonder and then to reason. She had cause for wonder for she alone, it appeared, produced the child. She did not connect man's hedonistic pleasure in his rutting season in the early spring of the year with the change in her own person, nor did he. Instead she thought that the swelling of her body had some-thing to do with the burgeoning of leaf and tree everywhere about her. This, she surmised, came from the warmth of the returning sun. It was the sun, she decided, that began the new life in her, too. But how, she asked herself, was this affluence carried down from the sun to her? The pains

118

of growing thought in her primitive mind were severe and she could use only the simplest, most concrete terms, reasoning from what she saw. It was the birds, she guessed, who brought the divine force to her, and every birth was a virgin birth. The ancient myth of virgin birth persists in all religions, even today. How many are the tales of lovely girls, who going forth to wash clothes at a pond, or to gather fagots in a wood, are impregnated by gods of river and forest! And the bird, too, lingers on in folk tale and religious story. The stork still brings the baby in some parts of the world, and the dove of peace, even the dove who came back to Noah's Ark bearing a living leaf in its beak, and the dove which is the symbol of the Holy Ghost, testify to the place of the soaring bird in early thought and wonder.

While woman thus forced the growth of a reasoning, thinking mind inside her skull, man continued his ways as a jungle child, a happy warrior, thinking nothing. He had no need to rack his brains beyond the cunning necessary to catch his prey. He, like the woman, lived alone at first until he found it better to hunt with a gang of his fellows, just as she found that it was better for her to live in a group of women for the mutual protection of the children. For the sake of the children woman devised shelter, and thus was the first architect and city builder. But man was useful, indeed necessary, for bringing in the food and fuel, and to reward him woman allowed him the strange hedonistic pleasure he took in her connection with him. Neither man nor woman knew the meaning of their mating. Lagging far behind woman in the development of brain and encouraged by her need of his brawn for heavy work and hunting, man was only woman's slave. Perhaps dim memories still haunt his subconscious and provide the basis for his continuing fear of the female and his resentments against her—who knows? Meanwhile, woman devised a philosophy of life for herself and the child whereby she not only became ruler and creator in the arts as well as in life but, believing that she alone had communion with divinities through bird and sun, she proclaimed herself alone the priestess, the mediator between divinity and man.

When did this supremacy of woman end? Bluntly, it ended when man began to suspect his part in reproduction. When and where the truth first dawned upon the male mind we do not know but its effect was devastating upon woman and totally changed the emotional and mental nature of man. He rose up from his lowly position. He asserted his indispensability. The process took centuries, for he found no way of proving what he surmised. But the more difficult the proof, the more urgent man became, until by Plato's time, he was articulate and the conflict between man and woman was in the open. Imagine the confusion in woman's mind when she could no longer insist upon herself as the sole source of life, or that her relationship to the divinities was hers alone! Her world went askew, she was overwhelmed. The monster of brawn that she had bred for his strength and his service to her household now was easily her master. Might became right and she shrank from her own creation. Though the physical fact of man's share in reproduction was not scientifically established until less than a hundred years ago—by a German scientist, von Hertwig, in 1875, to be exact, who proved biologically that the two cells, male and female in fusion, create a third being—yet man empirically was sure of his own importance long before. His next concern was to insure the fathering of his own children, and to that end he began to segregate his woman. Man in China insisted upon woman binding her feet so that she could not wander, and could be kept at home and guarded against other males. In India at about the same time women, who had always performed the sacrifices at the altars and composed and sung the religious music, were locked into their houses, the change hastened by the arrival of the conquering Aryans.

When man undertook the claim of superiority, however, he was soon beset with responsibility. Woman, accustomed to rule, was not as tractable as she is now after centuries of subjugation, and so much trouble did she cause man that he began to consider her the source of all his woes, for in spite of his complaints against her he was still at the mercy of his sexual hungers, which she alone could satisfy. He was in the ignominious position of needing her and having to plead with her or bribe her or force her to yield to him. This ridiculous situation he could not mend because of the recurrent times when he was ready to give her anything in order to purchase her yielding. The result of this was a mounting rage against her which took the form at last of declaring her the root of all evil. Women, traditionally leaders in religious as well as other fields, were no longer

120

allowed to be priestesses or even to compose or to sing religious music. So zealous were men to take over spiritual power too that in the great popular theatricals which, under their direction, the religious festivals now became, men themselves took the parts of women and minced their steps and spoke falsetto. "The whole romantic love life of the Athenian upper male society," says Sophie Drinker in her unique book *Music and Women,* "was transferred to boys, dressed in imitation of girls and idealized by the immature son of Aphrodite, the little Cupid. . . . The refined homosexuality of the Greeks, coincident with the taking over by men of women's rituals, choruses and music and dancing, is written large in the Dialogues of Plato. There one can see how it functioned to the last social detail. And in some of Plato's greatest passages on love and life, one can still feel it in all its decadence."

The arrogating male changed even goddesses to gods. Hymns which had invoked the goddesses now invoked the gods and "from the psychology of the Jews came the omipotent Father-God of our own religion today, with no daughter, no mate, and even no mother."

The end of one age and the beginning of the next has no definite moment in time or point in space. Centuries are needed for the merging of one age with another, and we are still in the age of woman's subjection to man. Modern woman is not in rebellion against man, nor is it likely that she will be, but her growing independence is manifest in her increasing recognition of the fact that, although man is equally important with herself in the reproducing of life and in the conduct of life in all its ensuing forms and functions, he is not more important than she is, and she is approaching the time when she will claim her place even in the policy-making centers of the world. She will refuse, one of these days, to carry out decisions made by man alone. Inheriting intelligence equally with man and having always her own special talents in intuition and in practical human relations, she knows that she has wisdom which she has no opportunity to contribute to human welfare. The knowledge is compelling her to action.

Lester Ward, the great American sociologist, said frankly, half a century ago, "I am tired of this one-sided civilization, of this false chivalry, this pretended regard which one sex shows for the other, while loads of putrid prejudice hang upon woman's neck. . . . The race can be raised up only when she [woman] is raised up. There is no fixed rule by which nature has intended that one should excel the other, any more than there is a fixed point beyond which either cannot develop further. Nature has no intentions and evolution no limits. True science teaches that the elevation of woman is the only sure road to the elevation of man. . . . Civilization demands this revolution. . . . Woman is half of mankind. . . . It is high time that all the forces of society were brought into action, and it is especially necessary that those vast, complementary forces which woman alone can yield be given free rein and the whole machinery of society be set into full and harmonious action."

I believe that as man ceases to fear woman, woman will gain in respect for man. She does not any longer, as she did in the days when she needed brawny slaves, admire the hairy chest, the monstrous thighs, the big muscles and the small brain cap. Today she admires the healthy male who is intelligent, who is mature enough to realize that she is a human being not subject to him, and wise enough not to want her to be subject, because life is at its height for man only when woman is her true self. And woman can be her true self only when she is free and is encouraged by man to exercise her freedom fully.

What is woman's chief responsibility today?

It is to prove to man that he need never fear her as she moves toward that complete equality with him in life which alone can mean freedom for them both together and alike.

And man's responsibility?

It is to forget the past with its dreams of old power and to look ahead and see the vision of woman as she could be, individually free and therefore a true mate. Merely to be man is not enough. Man must be partner in the creation of the child not only in the physical sense but in the development of the human being at highest level. Toward this happy end man must encourage woman to move, for she has been so long humbled by him that she cannot achieve it alone. She has lost herself in self-doubt. She must have man's encouragement to find herself again.

Thus, each helping the other to be free of old fears and memories, man and woman face their new paradise, a world where life is good for all.

122

O Mary, woman, it is not enough today, at Christmas, to sit there in the picture, so calm, fulfilled, at peace, the child encircled in your arms! The child must live. He must not die upon the cross or battlefield, or in the atomic holocaust.

O Joseph, man, come out of the shadow of your fears and stand beside the two you love!

The Christmas
Secret

"**M**erry Christmas, darling!"

David Alston heard his wife's voice from far away, somewhere on the edge of sleep. He opened his eyes to see her pretty face, framed in dark curly hair, bending above him. She was still at his side in the big double bed. He yawned mightily and turned over on his back.

"Not you, Peanut! Kids, yes—one groans and takes it—but a man's wife? That's cruelty—especially on Christmas morning!"

Peanut was what he had called her in the days when they went to high school together, here in this little town in the Green Mountains of Vermont, he carrying her books and she skipping along somewhere near his elbow. He was tall and she was a small little creature, dark to his blondness, gay to his gravity. Mary he tried to call her now, except in moments such as these. He drew her down to kiss her. She yielded with a nice readiness to enjoy, drawing back only when she became breathless.

"I couldn't sleep," she said.

"Why not, pray, when we didn't get to bed until one o'clock? I thought I'd never get those vehicles put together—three of them, God help me! I knew the boys had to have them this Christmas, but I didn't think Susan would want one, too."

"She wants whatever the boys have . . . David!"

"Yes? What now? Why the frown?"

"Do you think they'll see?"

"See what?"

"You know what I mean. Don't be stupid, darling, because that's only pretending."

He sat up and put aside the covers. "Now, Peanut, you know we said

126

we weren't going to worry. We said that from the very beginning—or as soon as we decided what to do about Susan. We said we'd take the chance."

"I know," she said. "I know—I know! But who could have imagined that she'd have the same platinum blond hair that you all have—you Alstons, and our own boys, for that matter? And the same electric blue eyes! They're so odd in that little Asian face!"

"Startlingly beautiful," he said. "Much more beautiful than any of us."

"No, just different," she said loyally. "If it weren't for the eyes and the hair, no one would know."

"There's the name," he reminded her. He was in the bathroom now, getting ready to shave. She was still in bed, leaning against the pillows she had piled one on the other. "Susan was my mother's name and my grandmother's."

"How do you suppose the girl in Vietnam knew that?"

"Richard must have told her. You remember the Sister at the convent orphanage told us that the girl was well educated—didn't speak much English but spoke French perfectly—educated by the nuns, wasn't she?"

"Yes. I have her last letter to Sister Angelica. The one before she—"

"Died. I know."

She climbed out of bed and went to the bathroom door. He saw her face reflected in the mirror, rosy with sleep, her hair a dusky nimbus.

"David!"

"What, my sweet?"

"Do you know she killed herself?"

He wiped his clean-shaven face on a towel. "Now, Peanut, we said we weren't going to solve that riddle. Sister Angelica said no, at first, because she was a good Catholic—and then—yes, perhaps, she did."

"I think she did."

"Why?"

"Because Richard is so attractive. If she loved him—"

"She loved him all right. Even Sister Angelica says that."

"Then she wanted to die when she knew he wasn't coming back."

"But he'd told her he couldn't marry her."

"Do you think she didn't hope?"

128

"He told her at the very beginning that he was engaged to Miranda. You know what the nun said. He was completely frank with her—even Thu Van herself didn't blame him—except for letting her love him."

"But he must have known a child was—"

He turned on her, his voice decisive. "He did not! I know my brother. It would have made a difference if he'd known about the child. Thu Van didn't tell him."

"How could she help it?"

They were interrupted by the door bursting open and two small boys rushing in. They stopped at the sight of the empty bed to chorus.

"Daddy, it's not fair!"

"You're not supposed to get up first on Christmas!"

He was in the shower now and he put out his head from behind the curtain.

"Your mother woke me up—your little naughty mother!"

"Mommy, you're naughty!"

"I know I am," she confessed. "What shall we do with me?"

They paused to consider this, their eyes big. Two little boys, she thought, adorable, beautiful, straight blond hair, electric blue eyes, Alstons both—Jimmy the elder and Ricky the younger, named for Richard after he had come back from Vietnam. How silent he had been in those days, how difficult, how torn by feelings he never divulged! They had been glad when, after months of indecision, he had suddenly decided to marry Miranda immediately. Now, of course—

"Come here, Susan," she said.

The little girl, a year younger than Jimmy, a year older than Ricky, stood hesitating at the open door, her great eyes, exquisitely shaped, the corners lifted, wide and watchful. She came forward slowly, doubtfully. She was a grave child, her perfect little face seldom changing. Mary put her arm about the slender figure in the pink pajamas.

"Merry Christmas," she said. "Merry Christmas to you and to Jimmy and to Ricky! Merry means happy. We'll all be happy today."

She kissed the little girl's cheek and went on. "Everybody get dressed. Yes—yes, I know—" she stayed the signs of dissent in the two boys, now jumping on the bed and starting a pillow fight. "We don't usually get

129

dressed first, but we're all awake, Daddy's nearly ready, and today we must be early because Uncle Richard and Aunt Miranda are coming. We can't be in pajamas when they arrive, can we?"

"Off the bed, boys," David ordered. "Obey your mother!"

The voice of authority, and they tumbled off the bed and ran gaily out the door. Only Susan stood motionless within the circle of Mary's arm. How much did the child understand? She spoke French, but shyly, her voice very soft.

"*Et toi, aussi, ma chérie,*" Mary said tenderly.

"Don't use French," David said sharply. "She must hear nothing but English. She's ours now."

"Come with me, Susan," Mary said. "I will help you dress." She paused at the door, the child clinging to her hand.

"Will you light the tree, David? We shan't be long. I'll not let the boys go downstairs first, because I want Susan to see the tree at the same time. I wonder if she's ever seen a Christmas tree?"

"Who knows?" David said.

"There's so much we don't know," Mary said.

Downstairs where the lighted tree was waiting, its base piled with gifts, he was thinking of all he did know. Sister Angelica had written voluminous letters, but there was more behind and beyond those letters—more even than she knew. He was ten years older than Richard and when their parents died in an airplane crash, he had tried to take his father's place with the sensitive, proud boy. Because of Richard he had postponed his own marriage. Somehow he had managed to keep the house going, working at the bank and earning enough to eke out the small inheritance their parents had left them. When at last he had married Mary it was to this home he had brought her. It was inconceivable that they live elsewhere than in this rambling white frame house with the green shutters, stretching from the parlor on the south, their living room, to the old barn at the far end, next to the big maple tree. Once a farmhouse, it was now on a wide, shaded street, the elm trees today laden with Christmas snow. To such a house, American for two hundred years, a little half-Asian child had come home. How strange the times!

The years before his marriage had been long and difficult. College and then postgraduate work for his younger brother had taken all he could spare, and Mary had waited for him in understanding patience. Richard was brilliant, he wanted to be an international lawyer and the training was expensive and arduous, meanwhile interrupted by military service in Vietnam. In that interval he and Mary had been married, but when Richard came back there were still two years of university to be paid for. Now he had a post in government in Washington, a beginning for a career that already promised success. Richard and Miranda had waited, too, for he had come back not wanting to be married at once, not until he had finished his education. Miranda's family had money, her father a supreme court judge, and Richard, always proud, had maintained that he would not marry until he could give her a home and a place in a community where she could be happy. Last year, now nearly a year and a half ago, the marriage had taken place and it was to all appearances happy. Then last Christmas the greeting card had come from Thu Van, written in French. "At this time of the blessed Noël, Richard, my beloved, I write to tell you I am still alive and always loving you. May the good God bless you, is the wish of my longing heart! I forget never. Your Thu Van."

The envelope had been addressed merely by surname—Monsieur Alston. He had taken it for granted that it was for himself until he read the card. He knew at once what it meant. Richard had loved a girl in Vietnam. This explained everything—his melancholy when he came home, his silence, his wish to postpone his marriage, everything that made him so different from the vigorous and articulate young man he had always been. He and Mary had long discussions of what to do. He had been inclined to send no answer.

"Certainly I shall not give this card to Richard," he had said in firm decision this day a year ago.

Yes, the card had been brought on Christmas morning, in the midst of the happy turmoil of opening presents and playing with toys. The postmaster, a neighbor, had brought a handful of belated letters. "I picked them up last night before I locked up and thought you'd like to have them today."

"Richard is only just settled in a splendid job," he had told Mary.

131

"Think what this would do to him if it were known—if even he knew that we knew!"

Mary, winding up a toy monkey for Ricky, had looked thoughtful. "I feel sorry for that girl," she said. "I do feel you should write to her and explain that you opened the letter, thinking it was for you. You could tell her that your brother is happily married and that you do not think it kind or useful to disturb his life, especially since he is no longer with us but lives in another city. Be honest with her. Say you aren't giving her card to him. Else her heart would break when there's no answer from Richard."

In the end he had followed her advice and had addressed the letter to the convent from whence Thu Van had written. The answer came not from her but from Sister Angelica. It, too, was in French.

"Monsieur," Sister Angelica wrote. "Your esteemed letter has come too late. Thu Van died here in the convent the afternoon of the day of Noël. She had been very sad after the departure of your brother, and since we love her as a former student we had begged her to come and spend the holiday with us. She brought to us her small daughter, born three years ago. This is your brother's child. When I saw the sadness of Thu Van, I inquired of its cause and she told me that your brother and she had a warm affair of the heart, but that he did not marry her. He does not know of the birth of this child. She preferred not to cause him grief by telling him. He left when she was three months pregnant. It is her noble nature not to wish to cause pain. Her position became difficult, however, since her family is a well known one. She was no ordinary prostitute, but a young woman of dignity as well as great beauty who met your brother, then a young officer, in the home of a French friend. It seems they fell in love immediately and at once the situation became passionate. To continue, she spent Noël with us here at the convent, keeping the child beside her all day. After the little one was put to bed, it is said by some that she took one of those swift and subtle poisons which these people of the East know so well how to use. Since she was Catholic, I doubt her capable of such sin. But perhaps! At any rate, the child's crying in the morning woke us early, and since it continued we went into the room and found the young mother lying on her pallet, dead. It remains now the question of what to do with the child. Is it possible the father would wish to claim her? Since he has a wife, it

132

may be that they would accept this child and bring her up as their own. She inherits her mother's beauty and something also from her father. Her hair is light in color, her eyes are very blue. She is of superior intelligence, as are most of these mixed children, we find. Instruct me, if you please, Monsieur, and I am your obedient servant."

He had handed the letter to Mary and she read it in silence. There had been no time for talk until that night when the children were in bed and then they were too tired to talk, too exhausted within by the emotions which all day they had not been able to share in the presence of others. But in the night Mary had waked him.

"David!"

"Yes?"

"I can't sleep."

He had waked instantly. "Then I won't sleep either."

"David!"

"Yes, my love?"

"We must take Susan."

It was she who had made up her mind. His thinking had been less definite—whether to leave the child in the convent, in her mother's land, or whether to give her to an adoption agency.

"But shall we be able to hide her?" he asked in consternation.

"We must take her for our own," Mary said firmly.

How well he remembered her clear soft voice coming out of the night, there beside him!

"She belongs to our family," Mary said.

"I suppose there are thousands of such children," he had said uncertainly. "They can't all be brought here. Perhaps she'd better stay there in the convent. We could send money."

"I'd never be able to sleep, thinking of her," Mary said.

For so small a creature she had an enormous will, cloaked in sweetness of voice and manner, but mighty within. Difficulties rose to his mind. "She may look like Richard," he demurred. "One thing is clear in my mind, Mary. I won't have Richard's life and career disturbed. It has cost too much combined effort, his and mine, to get him ready for his present place and his prospects are simply too promising to jeopardize. There is some-

133

thing more to consider than one child. Richard has a great deal to give to the country. He can rise as high as he likes and he's ambitious, not just to make a success of himself but really to serve in his generation. I will not have all this potential destroyed simply because of a half-Vietnamese child—even though she's his."

Mary had removed herself from his arms abruptly when he finished. "I think of her as half-American," she said clearly, "and therefore half ours. And her mother is dead. She killed herself because she loved our brother hopelessly. And he did love her in some fashion because he let her love him. There's an obligation. And the letter said that in Asia the child belongs to the father. The father is our brother."

The upshot of her determination was that they had begun the long process of adopting Susan, not as Richard's child but as a waif that might have been any waif, the child of an anonymous American soldier in Vietnam who might have been any soldier and whose mother, a Vietnamese girl now dead, had left her child in a convent.

The agency social worker had been doubtful and reluctant. "We must first see if we can find a Catholic family for this child of a Catholic," she had said.

They had gone through the long ordeal of waiting until in the end it was proved there was no Catholic family who wanted the child, at least within the area of the agency, and reluctantly Susan was given to them. It had taken a year, shorter by one week, and so, one week ago, Susan had arrived at the airport in New York and they had gone to meet her, he and Mary. She had descended from the plane, hand in hand with the hostess, looking lost and tearful. Mary had opened her arms then and the little girl had gone straight into that haven.

"I've always wanted a daughter," Mary had said through her tears.

The door opened softly at this moment and he saw Susan standing there. She had come downstairs alone. It was the first act of her own volition. Until now she had stayed where she was put, followed where she was led. Here she stood, transfixed at the sight of the glittering tree. Mary had bought her a red velvet dress with a wide white collar and had put it on her this morning. Above it her great eyes shone luminous and lit from within, and her straight blond hair hung to her shoulders. She came

134

nearer to the tree, softly on tiptoe, and gazed at it, her finger on her lip.

"*Joli,*" she whispered, "*très, très joli!*"

He watched her in fascination, surely the loveliest child ever born. He felt a foolish dart of jealousy that Richard was the father.

"Pretty," he said gently, "very, very pretty."

She turned her grave eyes to his face. "Pret-ty," she echoed. She had not allowed him to take her hand or lift her to his knee, clinging always to Mary, but now when he held her little left hand she did not withdraw it. They were standing thus, side by side, when Mary came flying down the stairs.

"Susan?" she called. "Oh, Susan!"

"She is here with me," he said.

Mary came in, breathless. "She came downstairs alone, David! I was helping Ricky. They're in such a hurry they can't get their shoes tied. So she simply came down alone!"

"I know," he said. "She stood there in the doorway. Then she came in. Look—she lets me hold her hand."

"Oh, the darling child!" Mary cried softly, and came in and sat down in a chair opposite the tree. "It's more beautiful than ever, because it's a special Christmas."

At this Susan withdrew her hand gently and tiptoed to Mary's side. Then, pointing her forefinger at the tree, she whispered.

"*Joli*—pretty?"

"Yes, dear." She lifted the little girl to her lap. "Oh, David, what if they see—and want her?"

He shook his head, unbelieving, and then was relieved at the sound of thunder on the stairs, the two boys leaping downwards to join them, pushing through the door and then running to the tree.

"Oh, look—"

"That's mine—"

"Stop it," David said. "We always sing first, remember? No shoving and pushing on Christmas morning, remember?"

They clasped hands then and stood around the tree and he led them

135

in "Tannenbaum, O Tannenbaum," and he saw Susan softly moving her lips, but uttering not a sound. She's doing her best, he thought, her very best to be one of us, bless her!

After that the day burst into its usual happy turmoil, the boys shouting and exulting, asking questions, demanding help.

"Dad, how does this work?"

"Dad, show me how to do this puzzle—"

"Gee, Mom, my sweater's neat!"

And throughout Susan sat on a small needlepoint stool, her gifts piled about her, opening them gravely one by one, examining each, and putting each in its place in a neat pile on the floor beside her. Ah, but the doll, of course! She had thought it part of the tree, it seemed, for last night they had set it on a branch near the top, securing it with a pink ribbon. Now Mary cut the ribbon and lifted the doll down, a girl doll, small enough to hold comfortably. She put it in Susan's arms and the child received the gift as a treasure not to be believed.

"*C'est pour moi?*" she asked under her breath.

"Yes, darling, for you," Mary said.

Thereafter the child, busying herself with the doll, and in a dream of pleasure, received her other gifts and without opening them put them on her pile.

"She has what she really wants," David said.

But Susan heard nothing. In the midst of the boys' shouts and laughter, in the midst of the exchange of gifts between the two adults, she sat absorbed, remote, undressing the doll, examining the rubber-skinned body carefully, then dressing it again.

"Thank you, sweetheart," David told his wife. "I've wanted this camera for a long while and I didn't think I should get it."

"So I did it," she said. "But how did you know I wanted a turquoise ring and bracelet to wear with my black velvet?"

"I guessed," he said.

They were exchanging a kiss, when they heard a voice at the door, a man's voice.

"A merry Christmas, I should say—if I'm to believe what I see!"

They looked up. In the doorway stood Richard and Miranda. They had not yet taken off their coats, and snowflakes lay on their shoulders and clung in Miranda's red hair.

"It's snowing again," she said. "We'll have to start home early. But Merry Christmas meanwhile!"

"Take off your coats," David said, going to meet them.

In the hall he helped Miranda with her coat, watching his brother the while, as he took off his own coat and hung it in the closet. He wanted to be in the room with Mary when they saw Susan. There might be instant recognition! Mary was standing in the doorway now. Don't try to hide the child, he thought. It's no use. We must be ready for whatever happens.

"Come into the kitchen," she was saying. "I must put the turkey into the oven. It's a monster—the biggest we've ever had—a sort of celebration for our little Susan. It's a special Christmas in this house. I was just saying so—"

She was shepherding Richard and Miranda toward the kitchen, an arm about each, and making talk as she went. "Come on, David, help me—I can't lift the bird."

So they were in the kitchen and there was a moment's respite—no, only a delay, and that was no use. The moment must be met and better to get it over with.

Mary was still chattering brightly. "I bought the turkey from old John Bright, next door. I always do. He raises the best turkeys in Vermont. I like to get a fresh farm-fed bird, and he knows exactly what I like."

Richard and Miranda stood smiling, watching, and Mary looked away. They were a beautiful pair, she thought, Richard so blond and Miranda a red-haired angel. They might make good parents for a child! Was David right in not telling them, in not leaving the decision to them? Has any person the right to make a decision for another, even his brother? In her place, were she Miranda, were she Richard, she would say no, let me decide for myself. But she was neither and Richard was devoted to his career, a dedicated man, a single-minded man, who, if his purpose were prevented, would be destroyed. That David had pointed out to her again and again.

"If it were I," he had said, "I'd want to know. But then I'm not a single-minded man. Nor do I want a career in politics. There's nothing I

137

couldn't leave, except my family. I'm a lawyer—yes, but a small-town lawyer. I can do a dozen other things—real estate, for example. Sure I love my home, and it would hurt me to leave, but then I wouldn't leave. I'd just say to the neighbors—yes, I was a kid in Korea once upon a time. Mary's my wife and she wants the child. But Miranda wouldn't want the child, Mary, you know that. She'd care about what people said. They'd both be broken up. I know my own brother—as fine a fellow as ever lived, but— well, I know him. He's on his way up, and I can't take the responsibility of blocking that upward way. People are sticky about a man's past, if he's dreaming of a Washington career. And I know there's no limit to Richard's dreams. He takes a look at the White House every time he passes, I'll wager that. And he should. He's the caliber the nation needs."

She had listened to this, had allowed herself to be convinced. Now she was unconvinced again. Ah, let the day take its course! If the child were recognized, then let it be so. If not—oh pray God, it's not!

"Come and see the children," she said brightly. The oven door was closed, the temperature adjusted. The gaily decorated kitchen, her work- shop she called it, all in red and white, was scented with plum pudding and spices. She led the way bravely, and David stepped ahead to her side.

"Susan is engrossed with her doll," he said. "Don't mind if she makes no response just now. She's a single-minded little soul."

That was another matter he was thinking—Susan's responses to these two. What if she felt impelled in some way toward Richard? Suddenly he dreaded that possibility as much as he had the other. What if there were mutual recognition? Nothing for it now but to face whatever happened. He led the way with Mary into the room again, deliberately stepping ahead of her to see the faces of the three who now met for the first time. Susan did not look up. She was undressing her doll again, folding each small garment carefully as she took it off. The boys leaped at their uncle.

"Uncle Richard!"

"Aunt Miranda!"

Jimmy, the elder, preempted the uncle, and Ricky, the younger, his aunt Miranda. She fended him off, laughing.

"Careful, Ricky—I've put on my best dress for you."

"Hi there, Jimmy," Richard said, sidestepping the violent embrace.

138

"Susan," Mary called. "Come here, dear. This is Aunt Miranda."

She went to the little girl, put the now naked doll into her arms and led her forward.

"Aunt Miranda," she repeated distinctly. "And Uncle Richard."

She glanced at David and caught his solemn gaze. Now was the moment.

"What a pretty child," Miranda said. "How do you do, Susan?" She leaned and touched her lips to Susan's cheek.

Ricky intervened. "Did you bring us presents, Aunt Miranda?"

"Oh, Ricky," Mary cried. "For shame!"

"For shame," Jimmy echoed. "But you always do, don't you, Uncle Richard?"

"Of course," the uncle said. "Only this time it's so big I have to have help. It's for both of you."

"I'll help—" Jimmy cried.

"We'll help," Ricky echoed.

"Richard," Miranda said sharply. "You haven't spoken to Susan!"

He had turned to the door but now he looked back over his shoulder, the boys clinging to his legs.

"Hi, there, Susan," he said. "All right, fellows, come on and help."

He went out to the car, David and the boys following, and Miranda sat down and smoothed her short skirt.

"We spent the night in Boston," she told Mary. "Richard wanted to push through in one day, but I can't take such a long day, especially with the next day Christmas, which, though delightful, is always a little tiring with children, I find. You really must come to us next year, Mary. You'd enjoy Washington. Such a lot goes on at Christmas."

"The children are used to being here at Christmas," Mary said gently. "But it's sweet of you to think of us. And we'll understand if it becomes too difficult for you to get away."

She was watching Miranda's stone gray eyes. No, she did not look at Susan. The little girl had gone back to her chair and was dressing the doll again, carefully unfolding each small garment and smoothing it out before she put it on the doll. Her bright hair fell straight on each side of her face, hiding it in shadow. But Miranda was looking out of the window. The snow was falling fast. She stirred in her chair.

139

"We must start back early," she said. "Else we'll never make Boston tonight. We reserved the hotel room."

"Vermont keeps her roads open very well," Mary said. Strange how quickly she and Miranda fell out of something to talk about! She was glad the boys were coming in again, followed by the two men. They were carrying a huge box.

"Look what we have," Ricky shouted.

"Electric train," Jimmy shouted.

"Wonderful!" Mary breathed. "It'll take the rest of the day to put it up."

"Where?" David asked. His eyes went quickly from one pretty female face to the other. Nothing had happened, he concluded. So far so good!

"How about the playroom downstairs?" she suggested.

"Oh, no," Ricky protested. "We want it here by the tree."

"Today," David said. "We'll move it tomorrow."

"Not too difficult after we have the thing assembled," Richard said.

He had not cast a glance at Susan, buttoning the doll's dress. The child had nimble fingers, Mary thought. She did everything with a careful perfection. Oh, really, she could not spare this child!

The snow fell softly through the morning until noon and then stopped and the sun slanted its way through the clouds and dispelled them. The scent of roasting turkey drifted through the house. The two women set the table with Mary's best silver and china and decorated it with sprigs of holly.

"Bonbons, as usual, for the children," Mary said, "but when they pop I hope Susan will not be frightened."

"She has not left off playing with that doll all morning," Miranda said, "I wish I'd had time to get the child a present, Mary, but we didn't get your letter saying she was here until Christmas Eve and you know what it's like to shop then."

"She doesn't miss it," Mary said.

"A queer-looking little thing with that Asian face and that light hair!"

"We think she's beautiful," Mary said.

"She doesn't talk much, does she?"

140

"Of course she does—perfect French and already beginning in English."

"Was she homesick?"

"No. She was told she was coming home—to us, here."

"What about her mother?"

"She's dead."

"Are there a lot of these children?"

"Many, we're told."

"So that's what our men are so busy about abroad!"

"Not all of them, I'm sure . . . Does Richard like his salad before or after turkey?"

"He doesn't like salad, period. Remember?"

"Ah, I'd forgotten. Now everything is ready, I think. I love Christmas dinner."

"I'm sorry you can't have it at night."

"Oh, we always have it in mid-afternoon as you know—for the children. They get too tired playing all day and then a big dinner—"

Idle talk, she thought, but somehow there was never much else to talk about with Miranda. But perhaps she was to blame, for Miranda had been a writer for a woman's page before she was married, and she, Mary, had never been anything but David's wife. Did she feel a slight inferiority to this smart woman from Washington? No, she did not!

"Dinner!" she called. "The turkey can't wait."

They came out then to the dining room, the boys reluctant to leave their toys.

"We have the engine attached," David reported. He lifted Susan into her chair, "and this afternoon we'll get the train moving. You must have spent a pretty penny, Richard.

"It was fun," Richard said briefly.

"A beautiful set," David said.

He glanced at Mary and shook his head slightly. Nothing—he conveyed to her inquiring eyes—nothing at all. He didn't look at the child.

"Everyone sit down," he said. "And no one may talk while I carve the bird. It takes concentration—and skill—and loving care."

"What's loving care, Daddy?" Ricky inquired.

141

"It means to go slow and take it as it comes," David said. He sharpened the carving knife meticulously and then proceeded to his yearly task. The first slice fell away, brownskinned on top and white inside.

"Perfect," he said.

He proceeded, all eyes fixed upon him as he performed. All eyes, that is, except Miranda's. She was gazing at Susan, who sat at Mary's side.

"I declare," she said suddenly, "that child looks enough like the boys to be their sister, the same blond hair, same bright blue eyes!"

Richard looked at Susan. "You're right," he said. He laughed. "And don't look at me, please, Miranda! There were thousands of American boys over there and most of them had blond hair and blue eyes."

"Anyway, the face is entirely different," Miranda said indifferently.

"It certainly is," Richard said. "There were plenty of those faces over there, too—those Vietnamese girls all looked alike to me."

Miranda laughed. "Thank God for that!"

"Thank God, anyway," David said, gravely. Again his eyes met Mary's at the end of the table. Steady, he was saying to her, steady now.

"Here's your plate, Miranda," he said. "You're the first to be served."

She took her plate, forgetting the child, and neither she nor Richard saw what Susan did nor heard what she said. Under Miranda's half-idle stare she had put out her hand to Mary.

"Prenez hand, maman," she whispered.

"Of course, Susan," Mary said, and putting out her own hand, she clasped the small searching hand.

142

Nineteen
Stockings
by the
Chimneypiece

This is the hour, unique in the whole year. Twenty-seven times the calendar has rolled around the circle of months to this hour of Christmas Eve. It is always the same and always different. The blessed sameness is in the old house which is our home and the Christmas tree, the gifts piled beneath it ready for tomorrow; it is in the quiet of the night when all are asleep except the two—or, as now, the one, myself; it is in the great stone chimneypiece by which I sit and the row of stockings hanging there. There have always been the stockings at this hour. The only difference has been in the number and the sizes.

They are limp and empty at this moment, but I shall fill them. And while I fill them, my mind, as always, goes back over the years when in this room, by this chimneypiece, we have filled the children's stockings. It is the final preparation for Christmas. Even when the children grew big enough to scoff at Santa Claus, even when they were big enough to go away to school and then to college, we never let them share this last hour of Christmas Eve and the filling of the stockings. This was our hour, the hour of recall and reflection, of private laughter and tenderness. We remembered, as I remember tonight, the incidents which made up the year so soon to be ended. We compared the children of this year with what they were the year before, the stockings bigger. How can boys have such enormous feet? Have we enough to fill them? These were annual cries. We always had enough, however big the feet were. And how small they were at first! There are still small ones, and the smallest now belongs to the newest baby, the tiny son of my daughter. And the row of stockings grows longer, five little stockings belonging to five little boys, and three little stockings belonging to three little girls, all the children of my children, hanging

between the long stockings of their mothers and the big-footed socks of their fathers. Somehow each stocking looks like its owner, the boys ranging from the newborn baby to a couple of six-footers, and the girls—well, girls come in all sizes, too.

Here beside my chair are piled the gifts that I shall put into the stockings. The logs are blazing in the fireplace, and in the library next to the living room someone who should be in bed is playing Christmas carols softly, with the sweet intent, I am sure, of keeping me from being lonely. For I refuse to have anyone with me now for this hour. The tradition in our house has been that on Christmas Eve, for stockings, the parents are Santa Claus, and since I am now the only parent, I am Santa Claus. Nineteen piles of gifts on the floor beside me—each carefully wrapped, the size commensurate to the stocking. Inexpensive gifts, of course, amusing rather than valuable, but I like to put one unexpected gift into each stocking, something small enough to fit the toe, but unusual enough to inspire the last search. A ring for a girl who thought she would not get a ring this year, a pair of earrings for a young mother who lost an earring last summer that a baby tugged off and threw in the grass, a gold pencil for the young man with a new job, a silver spoon for the middle-sized baby who believes she can feed herself better than parent or grandparent can do it, widespread food notwithstanding, a watch for a little boy who has just learned to tell time—such things are the treasures.

Everything is wrapped and, if possible, my time permitting, that is, a nonsense verse or a message of love goes with each gift. Some years I am full of verse; on other years I cannot find a rhyme however I search my brain. The children, large and small, take me as I come and they are philosophical about it. Children learn to be philosophical about their parents, for which I am grateful. It is a holy experience to receive into one's arms a newborn human being, but sometimes I think that the highest experience of all is to look a full-grown man or woman in the face and recognize the mature human being that once was the newborn child. A new communication is established and upon equal terms. The satisfaction, the sheer human comfort of it! Next to the primary love betwen man and woman, I know of no other emotion as deep as that which parents feel when they know their children are grown men and women, ready to take their share in life's work.

146

The babies' stockings are full now. I have been busy all this while, half remembering, half thinking, and in between listening to the music from the other room.

"What Child is this—on Mary's breast—"

We sang the carols as every family does, every year, and we sang them again this year around the piano, the young mothers holding their babies, the young mothers, whose mother I am, and the babies listened, wide-eyed.

The middle-sized stockings next, and these belong to my three youngest daughters, those whom the world has given to me, one from Germany, two from Japan, fathers American soldiers, beautiful world-children who by some good fortune for me found their way to this house and to me as their mother. Sixteen, fourteen, and thirteen, and a ring goes into the toes of two stockings and a gold thimble into the toe of the third, for the one who likes to sew. "No candy this year, please, Mother"—and so no sweets to these fastidious three who are beginning to know they are pretty. I put in the lipstick for the eldest and next year I shall have to put in a lipstick for the next one. Fifteen is the beginning of such decorations in our family, but a necklace goes in for each one, a silver handwrought necklace bought in Darjeeling, India, when I was there visiting the Tibetan refugees last spring. They are brave people, working hard to support themselves though exiled from their beloved and beautiful mountain country. I write a little message to go with the necklaces.

"Wear this with reverence for the pair of hands that worked so carefully to make something beautiful."

I am glad, too, that I bought the Tibetan jackets for the little boys and the gay Tibetan dresses for the tiny girls. I am glad I bought the hand-wrought brass candlesticks for the young married ones, I am glad I bought the two fine rugs for myself. I want to remember those noble people working to begin life again, anxious not to become a burden to their Indian hosts. Now at Christmas here in my home, in my country as yet undisturbed by war, I want to remember them. Let me never forget! Peace on earth, goodwill to men—

Ah, here is a treasure for my tall dark-eyed daughter, an emerald, rough cut, from India. She is clever with her crafts and she will set it into a gold ring or perhaps a clip. That goes into the toe of a very long stocking, so

147

long that I wonder if I can fill it. A fan from Japan, that helps, and then the nonsense things, and last of all a paperback book for the top. It is of course essential that every stocking must appear to bulge and certainly to overflow at the top. Dolls, of course, for the tiny girls, little dolls, not competing with big ones under the Christmas tree, and small trucks for the small boys, not competing with large vehicles tomorrow, and for the older ones the paperback books that curl up nicely, or any other such objects that protrude pleasantly from stockings. Candy canes always, for what is a Christmas stocking without a candy cane, red and white striped peppermint, harmless to all alike?

The value of stockings is apparent on Christmas morning when the older folk must get breakfast ready, a simple breakfast, remembering turkey and plum pudding later, ample in numbers, however, for while the table is set, orange juice and eggs and bacon and so forth in preparation, the stockings are unpacked. The little ones concentrate on the delightful task, and the older ones perform the same task en route between table and stove. By the time we sit down the stockings are limp again, and between sips and mouthfuls we exclaim and compare and the little boys swallow with dangerous haste so that they can get down on the floor and run their cars.

But that is tomorrow morning and it is still Christmas Eve. I finish the last stocking and hang it on the chimneypiece and sit down in the big chair to survey the noble work. A fine array, each year more stockings than the last, and peace descends. It is almost midnight. I wait, as we always did, until I hear Big Ben from London. The logs are a mass of coals, crimson under the gray ash. The music comes to a close in the other room and the one who made it tiptoes in and curls up beside me on the floor. I put out my hand and she takes it. Mother and daughter we wait. Midnight. Across the ocean we hear the bells in London. Christmas Eve is ended again for another year. I refuse the mist of sadness that might envelope me if I allowed it. Tomorrow is Christmas Day. This silent room will be filled with life, new life, life renewed. Another Christmas, for this world in peril. A trembling peace and goodwill too scarce, but, thank God, another Christmas!

A Certain Star

He woke at dawn this Christmas morning. For a brief instant he could not remember where he was. Then the warmth of childhood memory crept into his drowsy mind. He was here at the farm, in his old home, the broken rafters of his old room above his head. It was yesterday, only yesterday, that he had insisted upon this homecoming and against the subdued but massive revolt of his family he had carried it through.

"Oh, Dad," his daughter Anne had wailed. "Go to the farm now? On Christmas Eve? But we've planned—"

She had protested with such sparkling anger that he had turned on her with like anger.

"It's been years since I asked anything of you!"

His son spoke. "I have a date, Dad."

"You'll break your date, Hal," he had said firmly.

He had turned then from his two mute and furious children to Helen, his wife.

"Christmas has departed from this house," he told her.

She had smiled patiently. "I'm used to your large announcements, darling. And things are about as they have been, since the war ended. Everything's changed. It's inevitable."

"The foundations don't change," he had insisted. "We must get back to being a family. I'll have the car ready in an hour."

He was aware of the command in his voice. He had grown used to command during the war, and no less in these years of continuing atomic research. He was accustomed to obedience in his great laboratory of scientists and he did not stay to hear more protest in his house. And

knowing his punctual ways, they had assembled in an hour, and in total silence, for the long drive to the farm.

Well, they had obeyed him, at least. They were here together, miles away from late dancing and much drinking and the time-wasting frivolities that he detested. And it was Christmas. During this day surely he would win them back again. For he had lost them somehow during these years which had been absorbed in his work.

His name, his fame, Arnold Williams, nuclear scientist, one of the top three in the world, had overwhelmed them—and, to some extent, him. Scientists of every country turned to him for advice and argument and, compelled by the rapid growth of knowledge, he had dedicated his whole being to his researches.

This was his duty, of course, during the war, when his experiments had belonged to his government, but the line between duty and the pleasurable excitement of successful work was not so clear after the war ended.

While he pursued his separate way, his children had grown up, and Helen was certainly older than she should be. The old joy between them was gone. Yesterday, in his own home within easy distance of his laboratory at the university, he had suddenly realized that whatever was going on, in spite of last-minute shopping and an artificial, modernized tree, it was not Christmas. . . .

He remembered Anne, his daughter, so pretty, so feverish, not at all gay, flying to the telephone, always to be disappointed. It was never the right voice. . . . So whose was the voice for which she listened? Oh, Anne, beloved child, it was for her sake above all that he wanted to be alone today with his family. . . .

And what of the star? On Christmas mornings, when he was a boy lying here in this bed, there had been a certain star, high over the barn. He saw it always when he rose, earlier than usual, so that he could get the milking done before they opened the doors to the parlor where the Christmas tree stood. The Christmas Star! He threw back the covers and leaped out of bed—nonsense, probably, for the star might not be there now.

As he fumbled in the closet for his old clothes, it occurred to him that in a way this star was responsible for the direction of his life. It had led him to the heavens.

152

"What do you want for Christmas, boy?" His father had asked the question the year he was fourteen.

"I want a telescope," he had said.

His father had stared at him, his small blue eyes sharp and inquisitive above his ragged beard.

"What for?"

"To look at stars with."

His father had grunted, without sympathy it seemed, but on Christmas morning there was a mail-order telescope under the tree. It was the only gift he wanted. Impatient for the night, he had been compelled to wait until darkness fell. Then lifting his telescope to his eye, he peered at the star. What disappointment! It was larger, more glowing, but as far off as ever.

The next day, in sheer experiment, he had looked at the sun, and to his astonishment he saw spots upon it, and this had led to the buying of a book, an introduction to the sky, and so had begun his interest in cosmic rays.

He was dressed now in ski pants, sheepskin coat and fur boots. He slammed the door as he left the room, then winced, for Helen was still asleep, he hoped. If he had waked her, she would be patient with him, as indeed she had always been ever since his dark prowlings (begun long ago because his famous hunches came by night as well as by day) made it necessary for him to sleep alone. He could bear no interruption when he was seized by a theory and knew no peace until he had pursued it.

"When you marry me," he told Helen the day they were engaged, "you don't marry a man. You marry a sort of—of monster."

She had only laughed. Then one day during the war, when they were living in a barracks at Los Alamos, she had looked at him thoughtfully.

"What does that look mean?" he had inquired.

"Perhaps you *are* a sort of monster," she had said.

He had laughed, but the words came back to him now as he stepped outside the kitchen door into the darkness. The cold was solid enough to cut, the colder because the house was warm. He had put in an oil burner

153

years ago when the children were small, but when he was a boy there was only the huge wood range in the kitchen. It was still there, for memory's sake. . . .

The snow creaked under his boots as he walked toward the barn. The sky was clear, the stars luminous and twinkling through the icy air. He looked up, searching the heavens. Ah, his star was plain! There it hung over the ridgepole of the barn, not so large as he had imagined, but unmistakably the same.

The years had painted it bigger and more golden than it was now, or perhaps his boy's imagination had seen it so. Yet there it shone, steady and true, as he had remembered it.

His feet found the familiar groove in the path under the snow and as he stood in the windless air the old wonder came flooding back again, the wonder of the universe. He had known it years ago, distilled through the single star. He had lost it in the hurry and excitement of his youth, in the years when he had been working for a living by day in the laboratory of a great industry. In his own small laboratory, by night, he had explored the secrets of the explosive rays of the sun, and using his meager holidays he had made pilgrimages to Einstein in Germany and Rutherford in England.

Skeptic and daring, he had wandered far from this humble place upon which he now stood to gaze again at a star on Christmas morning. He had been a proud and argumentative man, until the day when he had found terror and a new humility in the nucleus of an atom, laid bare before him in a hidden place in the desert. Infinite energy, encased in a shape so small that eyes could not see it!

Yes, this star upon which he now gazed had guided his life. What next? Where would the path lie from this Christmas morning?

He shivered suddenly and remembered that he was standing halfway to his knees in snow. It had fallen during the night, the soft stuff clinging to every branch and twig, and the air from the lake was icy. He turned reluctantly and followed his own tracks back to the house and into the kitchen.

The light was on when he opened the door and Helen, wrapped in her red flannel bathrobe, was standing at the gas stove, making coffee.

"Merry Christmas," he said and kissed her cheek. "Did I wake you?"

"You're as cold as a snowman," she said, rubbing that cheek. "And you didn't wake me. I couldn't sleep."

"Christmas in your bones?"

She shook her head. "I don't sleep as well as I used to." She set two cups on the table and poured the coffee. "You want breakfast now?"

"No, but I'll have coffee."

They sat down. She sipped her coffee slowly, but he took a hot gulp. "That's good—I was cold all the way through."

"What were you doing outside at this hour?" she asked.

"What would you say if I told you I went out to see a star?" he replied.

"It's been a long time since you were interested in stars," she said.

He glanced at her. She looked too tired, this slender wife of his. "Maybe we shouldn't have come here to the farm. Maybe it's too much for you. Don't you feel well, Helen?"

"I'm all right," she said. "Just getting old, I suppose."

"Nonsense! You're worried about something."

She got up to make more coffee. "I heard Anne crying in the night."

He stared at her in consternation. "Why should Anne cry?"

"They don't say anything," she told him. "You know they never say anything nowadays. One doesn't know what goes on in anybody."

She threw him a strange, sad look which he did not comprehend.

"Anne seemed perfectly willing to come here yesterday," he reminded her. "She was more willing than Hal was—he had a dance or something."

"They both had parties." She stirred her coffee thoughtfully. "It isn't like Anne to give up so easily—not if she wants something."

"That's true."

Anne never gave up easily when she wanted something very much. So yesterday obviously there wasn't anything she wanted very much.

"I hope she wants the bracelet I've bought her for Christmas," he grumbled. "It cost enough."

"I don't know what they want any more. Everybody's changed somehow." She sighed and began sipping her coffee again, holding her cup in both hands as though they were cold.

155

He examined her face, still so pretty in spite of its pallor. It had been a long time since he had seen her in the morning before she made up her face. He was an early worker, and she slept late.

"Are you all right?" he asked again.

"Tired," she said. "My time of life, maybe."

"Woman's retreat," he declared. He got up and kissed her cheek. "Remember how you used to climb Mont Blanc with me when we were measuring cosmic rays? That wasn't so long ago."

She smiled faintly and did not reply. He tousled her hair to tease her and she caught his and slapped it gently. "I'll bet that your Christmas presents aren't wrapped."

"You're wrong! I had them wrapped at Tiffany's," he said.

She looked shocked. "Did you get everything there?"

"Everything," he said, "and when I said I wanted them gift-wrapped, the clerk said stiffly that the usual Tiffany wrapping *is* a gift wrapping."

That made her laugh and he felt victorious.

"And now," he said. "I am going upstairs to the attic to bring down my precious parcels for the tree."

"Why on earth did you take them to the attic?" she inquired. "The children won't snoop—you forget they're grown up."

"Habit. Before I knew it last night I was in the attic, putting my small expensive packages in the corner where we hid Anne's doll house and Hal's bicycle . . . How many years has it been since we spent Christmas here?"

"Not since you fell in love with the nucleus of an atom," she said. There was a glint of old mischief in her blue eyes. "I wish I knew the enchantment in a nucleus!"

"Ah, there's enchantment!" he retorted. He left her then and climbed the stairs to the attic and found his gifts in the brown paper bag in which he had thrust them for safekeeping yesterday. Halfway down the stairs again to the second floor he heard Anne's voice in the upper hall as she talked to someone—a man, of course.

"What's the use of my coming into town tonight? . . . Yes, I could come with Hal—he's got a date—but what's the use? It would be midnight before you could get away from your family and we'd have fifteen minutes

156

—well, half an hour then—and you uneasy all the time. What good is that?"

He heard the passion and the pain and, his heart suddenly aching, he saw her there at the telephone. She was still in her pink flannel nightgown, her yellow hair curling about her head, a mere child in spite of her twenty years. No man had the right to hurt this child he had begotten! How could he persuade her to tell his name so that he could defend her from the fellow?

"Anne," he said.

She hung up instantly. Then she turned and looked up at him with huge, startled blue eyes.

"It's early for you to be up on Christmas morning, isn't it?" he asked.

"I couldn't sleep," she said. "It's terribly cold here by the lake."

"It's just as well you're up," he said. "We have the tree to cut, Hal and I, and we'll trim it and get dinner together the way we used to do. I'll bring in some branches for you to decorate the house with—maybe some ground pine, eh?"

He deposited the brown paper bag on the stairs and came toward her.

"Feeling sentimental, aren't you, Santa Claus?" Anne crossed the hall to meet him and standing tiptoe, she kissed his cheek. "You're a sweet old thing," she said suddenly.

"Thank you," he said. "I haven't heard even that for a long time."

"I haven't said anything to you for a long time," she agreed. "You've been away somewhere these ten years, haven't you?"

She was tracing the outline of his eyebrow with a delicate forefinger.

"It's you," he said, capturing the forefinger. "You've grown up without asking me. I get only glimpses of the daughter I used to have."

All the same, he was thinking, if he hadn't insisted on being here today there would not have been even this interchange. She'd have been asleep in her bed, exhausted by dancing and carryings-on. She leaned her head against his chest unexpectedly.

"I wish I were little again," she whispered. "I wish I had never grown up!"

He pressed her soft hair. "Why, Anne—why, Anne—"

157

"Silly, isn't it!" She lifted her head and shook the tears from eyes that smiled up at him too brightly. Then running to her room she shut the door against him.

"Merry Christmas," he called after her, but she did not answer.

He opened Hal's door then. There, sprawled across the bed, lay his dear and only son—eighteen, a six-footer, handsome, brilliant—and a total stranger.

He tiptoed across the floor and looked down at his sleeping child. A man, this child—a child, this man. Tall, thin with youth, big bones, fresh skin and dark hair too long, here was his son, holding within the new shape of manhood a thousand memories of boyhood.

Hal it used to be who could not wait to get to the lake in summer, to swim, to fish, to sail. Twice he was nearly drowned in the deep, still waters, the first time swimming beyond his strength, the second time by a blow on the head against a rock when he dived. Twice he was saved, both times by his father. Three times, then, this son had been given to him alive, the first time fresh from his mother's womb.

Now he was a stranger who drove wildly into the night, who danced crazy dances with persons unknown, who came home, sometimes drunk, to break the hearts of parents. How could his son be saved? For inside that noble skull there was a brain worth saving. His own old professor at Harvard had written him about Hal. "If you can pull him through this pretentious youthfulness, this cult of 'beat,' you'll have a man."

Suddenly Hal opened his eyes and looked at him.

"What do you want, Dad?"

"Merry Christmas," he said.

Hal yawned. "Is it time to get up?"

"We have the tree to cut after breakfast."

Hal turned and burrowed into his pillow. "Okay—okay—"

He stood an instant longer, stifling his sudden impatience. Christmas, and the boy wanted to sleep! He remembered other mornings when Hal came into his room at dawn, shouting for the day to begin. And he had cut short his own sleep and had got out of bed so that his son could be happy.

He turned abruptly and left the room, closing the door just short of a bang. Patience! He was exhausted with being patient. Hal had no self-discipline. Why did men have children?

He went into his own room and stood by the window. The snow was falling in a flurry from a sky overcast with gray clouds. The star was gone.

The day was clear again when he and Hal went tramping through the snow after breakfast. His spirits rose in spite of himself. Filled with warm and nourishing food, encouraged by the sight of a pretty flush on Helen's cheeks, though it might be no more than the heat of the old wood range which he had insisted upon lighting in honor of the day, and softened by Anne's sporadic tenderness, he inclined his heart anew to this tall and silent youth who was his son.

"When I was a kid," he said, "we always had a white Christmas. We took it for granted. And I believe that you and Anne always took snow for granted, too, in the years when we came here for your Christmas holidays. Snow isn't so important in the city."

Behind him he heard Hal's crunching tread, but there was no answer to his small talk. He glanced over his shoulder, breathing out his frosty breath, and saw Hal's blank face. The boy was not listening. Then he caught his father's sharp glance.

"Did you say something, Dad?"

"Nothing important," he said shortly.

They tramped on. Why talk to a son who heard nothing? And he had a great deal to say to a son, a very great deal.

He longed to share with Hal something of his own life, the excitement of being a scientist in the atomic age when a scientist had suddenly become the most important man in the world.

In the past, isolated in his laboratory, working alone, often experimenting haphazardly, and usually in vain, a scientist had been scarely human, a magician, or a crank. Now, with the knowledge of the energy that was in the core of the universe, that infinitely small core, he was respected— and feared. . . . Did Hal dream of such things? There was no way of knowing, no communication between father and son.

He paused to examine the spruce woods in which they stood. The trees

159

had grown too tall. They would have to look for young growth beyond.

"How far are you going?" Hal asked.

"We must find a tree of reasonable size," he said. "We'll go to the edge of the forest."

"We could cut the top out of any tree," Hal said.

He shook his head. "I'm too good a woodsman for that. My father's ghost would rise. Kill a whole tree for its top?"

"It's getting late," Hal urged.

"What's your hurry?"

Hal stopped in the snow. "Dad, I want to get back to town by eight o'clock tonight."

He turned and faced his son. "One thing I asked of my family this Christmas—the one gift I really want—that we spend the day together here. And the day includes the evening. It will be six o'clock before we get dinner over. Then we'll have the tree."

He saw a strange look in Hal's eyes, a muted rebellion. If the boy felt that way, why didn't he fling out his anger? Once when he himself was eighteen, he had fought his father first with words, and then with fists. It had concerned a day, too, a summer's day when he had wanted to go to the state fair, and his father had forbidden it.

"Hay's fit to cut," his father had said roughly. "Nobody's goin' no-wheres."

"I'm going," he had said.

"Try it!" his father had shouted.

They had glared at each other. Suddenly his father had bellowed at him, "If you feel like you look, we'll fight it out—see who's the better man—"

They had fought, wrestling like bulls, young and old, and he had downed his father. He had watched his father get to his feet, pride and shame tearing his heart in two.

"All right," his father had said sullenly. "I'll make hay alone."

"I'm not going," he said and the two of them had worked side by side throughout the long hot hours until sunset. . . . Yes, that boy—himself—had been someone he could understand. Why didn't Hal defy him?

"You're the boss," Hal said. "Guess you'll always be the boss now."

He stared at his son's bitter face. "What the hell do you mean by that?"

160

"Just what I said. You're the boss. You've been the big boss ever since the war, haven't you? Atomic killer!"

He stared at the dark young giant, who glowered at him. Then rage ran over his body like fire and he hit his son on the jaw, a clean right-hander that amazed him. In the same instant he recognized pride in the blow—a low male pride that shocked him. His hand dropped.

"Hal!" he stammered. "Hal, I didn't mean—I don't know what got into me. But you called me an evil name. Still, I shouldn't have done it."

Hal pulled his handkerchief out of his pocket and mopped his face.

"Is it bleeding?" he asked casually.

"Yes, a little. It's a bad bruise. . . . What made you call me that name, boy?"

"It's what you are, aren't you? A sort of master killer—"

"No!"

Hal inspected the handkerchief spattered with blood. He rolled it up and put it back in his pocket.

"Okay . . . Let's cut the Christmas tree."

"Hal, I can't just let this pass."

"I said okay—okay."

"Okay, then!"

He was furious again and he stalked grimly ahead of his son for fifty paces. Then he stopped before a graceful young spruce.

"Here's our tree," he said.

"I'll cut it," Hal said.

He swung the ax three times against the trunk, each time missing the groove. Then he threw down the ax.

"I'm dizzy, Dad."

"Let me look at your face." He cupped his hand under his son's chin and examined the blackening bruise. "I'll ask you to forgive me for such an act on Christmas Day," he said abruptly.

"It's all right," Hal said. "I called you a name."

"Which I don't deserve," he maintained. "But rest yourself—I'll chop down the tree."

He struck four clean blows and the tree fell away with a long groan. He lifted the stump end and Hal took the top. In silence they carried it down

161

their tracks and across the meadow to the front porch of the house.

"I'll brush the snow off," Hal said.

"Let's go into the house and get warm first."

He led the way into the kitchen. The room was warm and fragrant with sage and roasting turkey.

"Hi there, you two," Helen called cheerfully. She was basting the bird in the oven, her face rosy and her hair a tumble of silvery curls.

"There's no oven like this one," she went on. "I wonder that we were ever willing to give up wood ranges."

"Wait until you have an atomic oven," he retorted. "A couple of minutes and your turkey is done. We sit down to the table and you press a button. We exchange a little small talk, pass the time of day, and the bird will be ready to carve."

Nobody answered. He was pulling off his boots and did not notice the silence. At the kitchen table Anne was polishing the old farmhouse silver.

"Any telephone calls?" Hal asked.

"None," Anne said. She looked up and gave a cry. "What's the matter with your face?"

"Your face," Helen echoed. She closed the oven door. "Why, it's awful!"

"I hit him," Arnold said harshly. He got up and drew a glass of water and drank it.

"I called Dad a name," Hal said.

Helen sat down on the kitchen stool. "Oh dear, oh dear—what is the matter with us—"

"A Christmas gift!" Anne said, and laughing hysterically, she buried her face in her hands.

"Anne!" he shouted. "Stop it! Stop laughing. Stop it, I tell you—"

He seized her shoulders and shook her. She lifted her face to him, broken with laughter or weeping, he did not know which.

"Are you going to hit me, too, Dad? Is that the sort of man you are now?"

He stepped back. "What do you mean?" he demanded. He looked from one face to another. "What do any of you mean?"

It was Anne who answered. She was the fierce one, the little fierce one

162

who flew at him and bit him one day when she was seven. In all justice, he had been compelled to spank her for unparalleled naughtiness because she had drawn pictures of lambs and daisies over his sheets of equations. The scars of her little teeth were on his thumb still.

"We don't know you," Anne said distinctly. "You're changed. You've become a stranger to us."

He contemplated these three whom he loved. For a moment he felt helpless and driven to escape. He thought of flight—anywhere to get away from them. Why had he ever left the comfort of his laboratory? Yet he could not escape them, wherever he was. He loved them, each of them differently and all too well. Wherever he went he carried them with him because he loved them. . . . And now he must face them as he had faced the other terrifying decisions of a scientist's life.

Should he pursue this knowledge to the uttermost, too, as he had pursued the quest of the energy locked in the nucleus of the atom? There had been times when he longed to escape that ultimate knowledge, yet he had been stern with himself. There could be no escape for the scientist.

Even while he knew that a secret energy could and might destroy the world, he had pursued the knowledge of it as his duty. It could, rightly used, bring life instead of death.

In a strange way love was like that, a power for evil or for good. Everything depended upon the human being. . . . So why were these three strangers to him now when he loved them so much? On this Christmas morning, he was conscious only of love. What could he say to make them understand?

He sat down at the kitchen table and looked from one face to another. They were watching him and he made himself gentle before them.

"Anne," he said at last, choosing her face among the three. "You're as honest as the Christmas star. I appreciate it. You say I'm a stranger to you, my family . . . and all the time I've been thinking that *you* were the strangers—you and Hal, and even you, Helen. I've felt lost here. But I've felt lost for a long time—in my own house."

Anne was embarrassed. He saw it. He must take it more slowly. "You've been busy, Dad—" she said.

"I've been busy, of course," he agreed. "Too much away from you all,

163

too busy about what I thought was my duty—my job. But I can't live without you, my—my dears, whatever I am."

He yearned for understanding but, searching their faces, he saw them still wary. . . . They didn't know him as he was now. Other memories crowded their minds. He could guess what they were thinking: That he'd make love to them, try to win them back again, prove that he was still the gay and tender father, the passionate lover and husband.

But he wouldn't plead. He spoke to Anne again.

"Go on being honest. . . . Why do you feel I am a stranger?"

Her lovely little face seemed to be shut tight against him. "People ask me how it feels to have a father who—who made the atomic bomb. They ask me what you're making now. And I say I don't know. Because I don't. You never tell us anything."

Hal broke in. "Don't blame Dad for the bomb. Whatever he had to do about that, I guess he had to do it. Besides, it's all over—long ago."

In the big, warm kitchen the delicious smells of pine branch and roasting turkey combined. Outside the day had changed. The sky was darkening again and snow was falling steadily in the windless air, great soft flakes. To the outer eye it was a Christmas scene as traditional as the turkey in the oven, the spruce tree waiting on the front porch.

He remembered it the same on every Christmas of his childhood, and yet today there was something in this house that had never been here before. A fear had unfolded itself, a human fear of a future—hideous but possible—because of what he and his fellow scientists had done.

And if the fear were here, was it not in every other house, in every other heart, a secret unspoken, a shadow unexplained? He who had discovered a miracle had failed to share it with these he loved. They knew only the fear.

He lifted his head. "Let me try," he said. "Let me try to explain myself. I think I understand why you are afraid of me."

Anne could not bear this. "Dad, not afraid of you, exactly. But nobody feels safe any more. That's why we rush around—we don't want to think about it. None of us do. . . . So we just keep rushing around, not thinking."

His wife took pity. "I know you can't help it, Arnold. . . ."

"I have a fear, too," he said at last. "The fear you have is a fear I share."

164

They were listening to him as they had not listened before. He was saying something new.

"Are you afraid of yourself?" Anne asked.

"No," he said strongly. "I know myself. Yes, I am changed, but not as you think. No one can discover the things I've discovered and not be changed. I am a humble man as I was never humble before. I believe in God. . . ."

He spoke the words simply, aware of their significance. He had never spoken the Name before. Agnostic and skeptic, he had taken pride in disbelief.

"Not the God of my fathers, perhaps," he went on, trying to be plain and not sentimental, "but yes, I believe in the eternal Creator, maker of heaven and earth. How can I not believe? I have met creation at work in the center of the atom—invisible, but full of purpose, immeasurable in power and energy. . . . I believe where I cannot see."

They were so still that they seemed not to breathe. It occurred to him now that he had never spoken to them of his serious thoughts. The days of their years together had skimmed by upon the surface of life. He had been too shy, perhaps, to uncover the hidden realities. And they had starved for reality.

They were relaxing, listening, Anne on the floor, her hands clasped about her drawn-up knees, Hal leaning against the door, hands in his pockets, and Helen sitting at the table, her head bent. She was listening, he knew, but skeptically, perhaps? Perhaps they were all skeptical.

He faltered. He tried to laugh. "Sounds big, doesn't it? Maybe I'm fooling myself . . ." He let the words trail off.

"I must baste the turkey again," Helen said suddenly.

He suspected, from the look on her too sensitive face, that the moment was more than she could bear. They waited while she opened the iron door of the oven. They watched while she dipped the fat juice with a big spoon and poured it over the huge bird. In these ways, he thought, were the vast, the small, mingled in their lives today. Christmas star and atomic fears.

She drew a glass of cold water, drank it and sat down again at the table.

"Go on, Dad," Anne said.

"I don't know how to go on now," he said abruptly. "It's true I've been away for years. Even though I sleep and eat at home a good deal of the time—I'm somewhere else. Maybe I can't get back. Maybe we'll never really meet again, you three and I.

"It's lonely, being a scientist—a lonely life. We don't make contact except with one another in our own world. That's why we keep going to conferences and meetings, I suppose—trying to find people who speak our language—with whom we can communicate through equations. . . . You've got to meet me halfway, you three!"

"Suppose we can't," Anne said in a low voice.

"Then I suppose I'll have to go my way alone," he said somberly.

Helen got up and went to the window and stood there watching the drifting snow. "We're all in the atomic age together," she said. "You got there first, that's all."

"That's very perceptive of you, darling," he said gratefully.

The telephone rang. Hal went into the hall to answer it and they waited.

"I don't know whether I'm coming," they heard him say. "I won't know for a while yet . . . I'll be late if I do come."

He came back into the room. He threw himself down on the shaggy rug before the kitchen range, crossed his hands under his head and stared at the ceiling.

"Go on, Pop," he said.

"I can't go on," he said to his son. "You'll have to take me on faith. You can believe in me whatever I do, or you can't believe in me. All I can say is that I have seen a vision as truly as those men of old who followed the star—the wise men. They believed that a child would bring in a new and better age . . . and so do I."

"Plenty of people were afraid of that new age, too," Helen said.

"Right again," he said, and again was grateful.

She had been peering out the window and now she went to the bread box and found a crust and crumbled it. Then she opened the window and put the crumbs on the outside sill.

"I see a belated wood thrush," she said.

"Herod tried to kill the child, remember?" This was Anne, remembering the old story.

166

He turned to her. "He wanted to stop the new age. But nobody can do that—nobody and nothing. There's no going back to what we were—Herod couldn't kill the child . . . and we can't destroy the creative nucleus of the atom. It's eternal. It's there. We have to learn how to use it—for good and only for good."

He got to his feet restlessly and began pacing the floor, from the window to the south to the window to the north while the snow drove white against the panes. The big old kitchen stretched the width of the solid house. And he mused aloud . . .

"I wish it could have begun differently—in peace instead of in war. I wish I could have lighted cities and made houses warm and perfected a fuel for wonderful machines that aren't even invented yet. . . . But it couldn't begin that way, it seems. First of all we had to stop a subhuman man from destroying the world."

He paused and faced them.

"You understand? Hitler would have destroyed us! He was after the bomb, too. We were only months ahead."

"But Germany had surrendered," Anne said.

"Japan hadn't," he retorted. "And there were subhumans there who wanted to keep on fighting. It's the subhumans we have to watch."

He was pacing the floor again. "The only thing I fear in life is the subhuman. I trust the energy in the atom—you can know it and learn to use it—it's predictable. And I trust a good man as I trust God. But the subhuman—no! He's the enemy—the only one we have. And he may live next door as well as across the sea. He might be alive in one of us—even in me!"

He stopped in front of Anne and jabbed his long forefinger at her. "That's why you're afraid of me!"

His hand dropped. "Good God, child—you *should* be afraid of me! I was afraid of myself this morning." He turned to Hal. "Son, why did I hit you?"

"Forget it," Hal said under his breath. "I was mad at you, too."

"I can't forget," his father said. "There's something subhuman in me, too."

He was talking aloud to himself, putting his soul into words this Christ-

167

mas morning. But they listened. Even though it was too much for them, they knew what he was talking about. Helen held out her hand to him and he grasped it. Anne laid her forehead against her hunched knees and he saw her body tremble. Was she weeping? He did not know.

Hal leaped up from the floor and clapped him on the back. "Enough talk! I guess we understand each other a little, anyway. . . . We'd better get the tree up, Dad. I'll drag it into the living room through the front door."

"I'll find the Christmas tree trimmings," Helen said.

She stopped on her way and kissed his cheek. But Anne sat crouched on the floor, her head bent. He glanced at her and went to the window and looked out. The snow had ceased to fall and between the wintry gray of the sky he saw lines of blue again. A variable sort of day, he thought, and it was not half over. Getting up early, even to see a star, was beginning to tell on him. And all this commotion in his family—who knew how deep it went? He had lost too much time to retrieve in one day.

And then Anne lifted her head and began to talk. "I've wanted for weeks to tell you . . . I'm terribly unhappy."

He felt his heart leap. Then he had not utterly failed!

"Tell me why you're unhappy, Anne."

"I've fallen in love."

He drew up the hassock and sat down within reach if she put out her hand to him.

"But that's wonderful," he said gently.

"It's not," she said. "I love someone who doesn't love me."

"Not possible," he declared. "I don't believe there's a man on earth who can't love you. Even if he's blind and can't see the way you look."

She laughed brokenly and scrambled to her feet. She came to him and leaned her cheek on top of his head so that he could not see her face.

"He doesn't love me enough," she said. "Not enough to give up anything for me—only enough to kiss me—and so on."

"And so on . . ." he repeated. "That's not enough, I agree."

"No," she said. "Because I love him too much. So it's got to be everything or nothing—Dad, he's married. So it's nothing."

"That's bleak," he agreed gravely. "That's very bleak."

She broke at his tenderness. "Oh, Dad, the world's empty!"

He pulled her to his knees, a child again as she used to be and a child still. She buried her face against his shoulder and began to weep soundlessly, as a broken heart must weep. No, she was not a child. A child sobs aloud. . . .

He held her, waiting. He could not throw out the usual snips and bits of comfort. You are only twenty—there are other men, young and handsome. This will pass, my child, this will pass. He would speak only the truth.

She lifted her distraught face. "Shall I ever get over this, Dad?"

"Never," he said. "One never gets over these big things. They stay in you. Other things will come—other loves. You'll live in them, too. You'll live in everything. We must—there's no escape from living."

Her head dropped to his shoulder again but she was not weeping now. He felt the heart in agony but her mind was working, her will assembling itself. She sat up and smoothed her hair.

"What would have happened to me if you hadn't made us come here for Christmas?" she asked.

"Tell me," he said.

"I planned to run away—with him—for a weekend. And this morning I couldn't. I heard you get up and go outside. I went to the window and watched you tramp through the snow and stand there by the barn a long time."

"I had to see the star again," he said.

"The star?"

He told her then of what the Christmas star had meant to the child he had once been, here in this old house, and how yesterday in the city he had longed intolerably to come back, to get his bearings once more by the star.

She slipped from his knees, no more the child. "That's what I need—to get my bearings."

"Sense of proportion," he said. "What's important and what isn't."

She walked to the window as he spoke and now she, too, stood looking out upon the snowy scene.

169

"Don't tell anyone about me, Dad—"

He was shocked. "How can you think I would?"

"I thought you might say something to Mother."

"You haven't?"

"No. She has enough to worry her."

"Something I don't know?"

"She thinks nobody knows. The doctor told me."

He went cold. "I should have been told at once, Anne."

"She didn't want *you* told, especially, and none of us until after Christmas. That's why the doctor told me. Somebody ought to know, he said."

"She doesn't want me told," he repeated, stupefied. "But the doctor ought not to have listened to her!"

"She wouldn't even let him give her the tests until after Christmas. That's why he told me—in case she didn't feel well meanwhile."

He groaned. "All these doors shut between us!"

She came back to him and put out her hand and he clasped it for comfort. "You've opened one door today, Dad. And one open door helps the rest of us. Now we can communicate."

"But will you?"

"I will—I promise."

She smiled at him, a wise and sad smile. Some of the brightness of youth was already gone from her face.

"You'll be all right," he said. "Not at once, but step by step, a day at a time."

"Yes . . ."

She paused and sniffed. "Dad—the turkey!"

She flew to the oven and he grinned and went away. Out in the hall he called, "Helen, where are you?"

From afar off, from behind a closed door, her voice answered indistinctly.

"She's upstairs," Hal said from the living room.

The tree was up and fastened in its stand and he was pounding a last nail. "She went up to get the tree decorations and she hasn't come down. Maybe she can't find the star for the top. She couldn't remember where she put it."

170

He did not wait for Hal to finish. Up the stairs he leaped and to her door. It was locked. He tried the handle again.

"Let me in, Helen!"

"Just a minute, dear."

Her voice came faintly through the panels, but in less than a minute she turned the key and opened the door. She did look faint. Her eyes were enormous in her white face.

"Darling, what is the matter?" he cried.

He took her in his arms and she clung to him without answer.

"Why did you come up here all by yourself and lock the door?" he demanded.

"I don't want to tell you," she whispered after a time. "I don't want to spoil our Christmas."

"It's a day for telling," he said. "It's a day for trust."

"I'm not well," she faltered. "Something is wrong with me."

He looked down at the beloved face, pressed against his chest. The eyes were closed.

"Why didn't you tell me?"

"I couldn't—you were so far away."

"You went to the doctor by yourself?"

"Yes." The word was a sigh.

"What did he say?"

"The tests aren't complete."

"Am I far away now?"

"No."

"Never again?"

"Never."

"I'm going with you to the doctor tomorrow—and I'm staying with you."

She lifted a face suddenly bright. "Oh, Arnold, will you?"

"And maybe nothing is wrong," he said, "nothing that can't be mended."

"I can believe it possible—now."

She looked up at him, in her eyes a trust renewed. He bent his head and

171

kissed her with a passion deeper than he had known in years. They were close again.

Downstairs Hal was telephoning.

"Hi, kid! Say, I can't get there tonight . . . No, not even late . . . I'm just not coming, see? . . . We're having our tree and everything."

The receiver slammed and he yelled up the stairs. "Dad—Mom—you two up there! Are you bringing the Christmas stuff down? And don't forget the star!"

They drew apart and smiled. It was impossible not to hope on this Christmas day. That indeed was the whole meaning of the star.

Christmas
Verities

It is a cold clear morning. Here in the mountains of Vermont, where I sit writing, we expect snow early, and last night it came, soft and silent, through the night. Beyond the big window by which my table stands, Mount Stratton lifts its white head high against a sky of burning blue, and near me, only the glass between the warmth of the room and the shining cold outside, the fir trees are layered with snow, each a perfect Christmas tree.

Well, I am ready for Christmas—materially ready, that is. Each gift is wrapped and labeled. My Christmas pudding, which stubbornly I still make myself, although I suppose puddings just as good can be bought in a dozen places, is steamed and enriching itself with time, awaiting the final hour at Christmas dinner. Holly wreaths hang at the windows and red candles gleam on the chimneypiece. Everything in the house is ready for Christmas—except, perhaps, the Christmas spirit.

I have always loved Christmas, a love born in the long-ago days of my childhood in far-off places in China. There, because we had to make Christmas entire within our own household, because there were no shops bright with ribbon and decoration, no silver tinsels and golden stars unless we created them, the Christmas spirit swelled early, strong and deep into our hearts. Love of our distant native land, love of the people who were our own but whom we did not know, mingled with the traditions of Christmas. It was easy, when we sang the carols of Bethlehem and the Child, to sing, too, of the land, so beautiful for spacious skies.

Now I am in that land and it is beautiful, the skies are spacious, the people no less dear for being well known. Most of my dreams have come true. I am a happy woman and happiness overflows into every relationship

174

and activity of my life. I have no complaints. And yet, this morning, as I wait for Christmas, I wait, too, for the Christmas spirit of this year of 1956. I do not yet feel Christmas in me, the spirit that alone infuses meaning into the gifts and the preparations, enriching the giving and the receiving on Christmas Day.

Let me search my memory while I wait. What is the difference between Christmas now and the Christmas of long ago? It is contained in the difference between the days of our forefathers, the age of the pioneer and the covered wagon, the age of the candle and the lantern, and this our age, the jet-atomic age. It has come so fast, the monstrous change. Within a lifetime, the span of a few score years, horse-drawn carriages have given way to swift motors and to rocket engines in the sky. Sleigh bells have become nostalgic toys, and on Christmas Eve their jingle will be drowned, likely, in the whine of a jet's afterburners. True, we shall sing the Christmas carols in the old way, the family gathered about the piano for memory's sake, but when the children have gone to bed, we elders will listen to great choirs of professional singers whose voices come to us by record or radio or television, and beautiful as their music is, something is missing there from the old melodies of Christmas. And lucky though we are as a family to own a spot of land where we can go out and cut our Christmas tree, this has become a rite and not a reality. The average family has no woodlot and instead will buy a tree at the store or from the man who goes through the new housing development near us with a truckload of trees. And even he does not see the woods but has hauled his trees from the railroad freight yard. Oh, we'll celebrate Christmas, just the same, but for some it will be only a day of too much food, too many gifts, and at the end, weariness. Where the spirit fails there is always weariness.

And the spirit fails, perhaps, because we are still tied emotionally to yesterday, so that today seems ephemeral and unreal. We have not put down deep roots—and we dare not, for tomorrow presses so hard upon this still unrealized today that roots will have to be pulled up again and yet again. Are there no verities left to us? Every thinking mind must ask the question. How shall we translate in terms of today's life the meanings which yesterday seemed eternal?

There are verities, and they are still eternal. In spite of every change and

176

through every change that is now taking place and will take place in the unimaginable future, the verities remain unchanged. Let me review them for my own soul, this morning before Christmas.

The verity of human beings remains. I gaze out upon the high white stretches of the mountain. It is the same, yesterday and today and forever. A tablet upon the mountain tells me that a century ago eighteen thousand people gathered to hear the political speech of one Daniel Webster, who spoke for freedom. Well, eighteen thousand people could not be mustered now to gather upon this mountain's flank. The children of those men and women have scattered over the earth's surface and their farms have gone back to forest. But wider thousands still gather to hear men speak of good government for a free people. The change has been only in the medium. The people, past and present, are the same.

Today, more than ever, with all the zest of their forefathers, the people search for good men and women to sit in the seats of government. Does it matter that the voice comes through a machine? I think not. Daniel Webster's voice floated down the air waves upon a mountain side and fell no more directly upon the listening ears than does the voice of the man who today addresses us. His voice, too, rides upon the waves of the air and with the same speed of sound, though the distance is magnified by thousands of miles. We, his listeners, judge his words and seek to know his mind as eagerly and as acutely as did those earlier men and women when they stood upon the mountain slope, to weigh the words and thoughts of Daniel Webster. We are the children of those people, their spirit lives in us and we bequeath that spirit to our children.

The other day I heard my son, turned twenty, say words which will comfort me for the rest of my life. We were disagreeing about something —what, I have forgotten. I was fearful, I suppose, as parents are, lest he act in some way I could not approve. It is hard for a parent to know the exact moment when a son is fully grown. Suddenly he turned a smile upon me. "Mother," he said, "you needn't worry. You've put a conscience in me and that's the most that any parent can do. Oh, I won't pretend! I'd like to be rid of it, once in a while, but I can't. It's in me for life."

I could let him go and I did. "Do what you think is right," I said.

Our forefathers put conscience into us, too, the verity of the knowledge of good and evil. It is a wonderful fact that while the peoples of the earth differ much in the ways in which they live and even in the ways in which they think, yet upon what is good and evil they all agree. A good man in any country is the same man. He is the honest man, the man of honor, the man who thinks of others when he thinks of himself, the man whom people can trust for magnanimity as well as for justice. This is eternal verity.

I am reminded here of a few sentences from Proust. Speaking of his friends, the Verdurins, he says:

"They are magnanimous, and magnanimity is, after all, the only thing that counts, the one thing that imparts distinction. You see, there are only two classes of beings: those who are magnanimous and the others; and I have reached the age when I must choose, decide once and for all whom I shall like and whom I shall despise, stick to those I like, and make up the time wasted on the others, never again leave them until I die. . . ."*

The magnanimous are verity. They also are to be found in every country, among every people. We need not fear the jet age nor the atomic forces so long as this is true. The fate of humankind is safe in the hands of the magnanimous. We have only to seek them out and never leave them.

And whence comes the magnanimous spirit? How is it conceived, how born, how bred? For answer I return to an ancient book of Japan, *The Heike*. There, among the stories of many people, is also the story of Saigyo, the monk who fled from life to escape the tortures of desire and ambition. Yet he had first to learn to love the life that he had chosen, for "he was prepared to declare that he who had not learned to love his own life could not love mankind, and what he sought now was to love the life which was his."

Here, I believe, is the verity of verities. Before we can be magnanimous, before we can be people of goodwill, and so bring goodwill upon this earth, we must love life itself. And how love life when its changes confound and confuse us, and the old ways of living are gone? The verities, I say, remain unchanged. People are not different from what they ever were. The good are still the good, and evil is evil. However, the standards

*A la Recherche du temps perdu, by Marcel Proust.

178

are wrenched this way and that until we feel that life itself is out of equilibrium; we have only to wait and equilibrium is restored. Good emerges again as good and evil is once more set apart. Storms and tempests may wreck a landscape but the wreckage is temporary. Sun and warmth prevail and life grows again and the landscape resumes its essential self.

The verities of the earth are great verities, second only to the truth of goodness and the human conscience. I have learned, when I cannot understand life for a time, to return to the earth. Again I am fortunate because I live in the country where the earth is beneath my feet and before my eyes day and night. But earth's verities can be as plain to see in a growing plant upon a city windowsill. The laws of life and growth proceed unchanging and unchangeable. As men have come and gone upon the mountain, they have come and gone everywhere upon the unchanging earth, living according to the same laws of life, both physical and spiritual, and the earth itself does not change.

Actually the change is in our knowledge of what has already existed since time immemorial. We may wish we did not know about the atomic forces which can destroy us, if we so allow. Was it not better, we cry, when we did not know? But there was never any time when we were not learning, when we did not know. When man first discovered fire doubtless he was terrified, doubtless he was shaken to the core of his being, overcome with the horror of the new and seemingly uncontrollable force. Yet he learned to control that which he has never yet wholly understood, for what is the meaning of this sudden transfiguration of dead matter into a living flame no one knows. We know the cause and the effect, but we do not understand the change itself, any more than we understand why, when certain simple materials, seemingly inert and certainly ancient in themselves, are put together within the framework of a formula we should then have the terrifying new force which we call atomic. The further we learn, the more we shall know, but the pattern is unchanging from the very beginning of time until time ends, if time can end.

Change, too, is verity, but change is always within the well-known pattern. It is still a truth, as the old preacher declared in Ecclesiastes, that there is nothing new under the sun. The elements of earth and mankind

179

remain unchanged. New formulas are discovered, new rearrangements of old forces, materials hitherto unknown emerge and take their place, but the elements remain what they were created, and mankind, men and women, pursue their endless course together.

Of man and woman the child is born, new and fresh in every generation, and yet eternally the same. When I contemplate such verity I am comforted by life's stability, by earth's unchangeableness. What has seemed new and frightening assumes its place in the unfolding of knowledge. It is good to know our universe. What is new is only new to us. It has been here always. It will be here always.

So Christmas takes its place as part of the unchanging pattern. The old ways change, but the spirit does not change. It does not matter what the gift is, because the giving and not the gift is the verity—the giving and the receiving. And the giving and receiving signify and prove that the spirit is not dead. In the humdrum of daily life it might easily be believed by the despondent, harried soul, which sometimes anyone is, that all is selfishness and coldness of heart, that love is lost. Then Christmas comes and in the symbolism of its giving and receiving among those we know and love and the unknown, the poor and lonely in every community, we find our faith renewed because our own hearts are warmed again to life and love.

Yes, we need Christmas. Christians have made Christmas, but in every religion everywhere in the world there are days which mean Christmas, days of renewal of peace and goodwill among men. The ways in which we express the day's meaning differ in time and place but the meaning never changes. The blessed Christmas spirit descends upon us even in this year . . . And so, God bless us all.